Family

DEC Recommended Practices Monograph Series

DEC Recommended Practices:
Enhancing Services for Young Children With Disabilities and Their Families

Environment:
Promoting Meaningful Access, Participation, and Inclusion

Family:
Knowing Families, Tailoring Practices, Building Capacity

Family

Knowing Families, Tailoring Practices, Building Capacity

DEC Recommended Practices Monograph Series

Division for Early Childhood
of the Council for Exceptional Children

Washington, DC

ISBN: 978-0-9905128-2-0

Disclaimer

The opinions and information contained in the articles of this monograph are those of the authors of the respective articles and not necessarily those of the Division for Early Childhood (DEC) of the Council for Exceptional Children. Accordingly, DEC assumes no liability or risk that may be incurred as a consequence, directly or indirectly, or the use and application of any of the contents of this monograph.

Published and Distributed by:

E-mail: dec@dec-sped.org
Website: http://www.dec-sped.org/

The Division for Early Childhood (DEC), a division of the Council for Exceptional Children, is an international membership organization for individuals who work with or on behalf of young children with disabilities and other special needs. Founded in 1973, DEC's mission is to promote policies and advance evidence-based practices that support families and enhance the optimal development of young children who have or are at risk for developmental delays and disabilities. Information about membership and other resources available can be found at www.dec-sped.org

Editors: Carol M. Trivette, *East Tennessee State University*, and Bonnie Keilty, *Hunter College, City University of New York*
Copy editor: Kevin Dolan
Cover and interior design: Kevin Dolan
Indexer: Jean Jesensky, *Endswell Indexing*
Typeset in Warnock Pro, Myriad Pro, and Calibri
Photos provided by iStock

Suggested Citation

Trivette, C. M., & Keilty, B. (Eds.). (2017). *Family: Knowing families, tailoring practices, building capacity* (DEC Recommended Practices Monograph Series No. 3). Washington, DC: Division for Early Childhood.

TABLE OF CONTENTS

Division for Early Childhood
of the Council for Exceptional Children

Download the DEC Recommended Practices
www.dec-sped.org/recommendedpractices

Working With Families
Today and Tomorrow

BONNIE KEILTY
Hunter College, City University of New York

CAROL M. TRIVETTE
East Tennessee State University

THE DEC FAMILY RECOMMENDED PRACTICES PROVIDE UNIVERSAL guidance for professional work in early intervention (EI) and early childhood special education (ECSE) that enhances the confidence and competence of families. We were interested in taking the leadership on this particular monograph because we believe in the importance and power of the Family recommended practices. We know that when practitioners implement the Family recommended practices with fidelity and in partnership with families, outcomes for children and families are better. We also know there are practitioners, including aspiring practitioners (i.e., students), who are unfamiliar with the recommended practices or how to use them effectively. There are others who struggle with applying the recommended practices in certain situations with individual families. And there are those who seek to continue enhancing their knowledge and skills by learning from other's work. For all practitioners as well as administrators, professional development providers, and researchers, we were intentional in seeking and selecting monograph contributions that highlight the recommended practices as the foundation for work with all families. Most particularly, we were interested in contributions that were purposefully situated in the following principles:

All families are unique. Recommended practice F1 clearly speaks to the uniqueness of each and every family and the importance that all interactions are "sensitive and responsive to cultural, linguistic, and socioeconomic diversity" (Division for Early Childhood [DEC], 2014, p. 10). EI/ECSE practitioners purposely seek to understand and appreciate the unique characteristics of each family to avoid erroneous assumptions. That way, practitioners can tailor their approaches

DEC Recommended Practices Commissioners

Mary McLean, chair
Rashida Banerjee
Tricia Catalino
Chelsea Guillen
Kathy Hebbeler
Anne Larson
Tara McLaughlin
Lori Erbrederis Meyer
Brian Reichow
Beth Rous
Susan Sandall
Pat Snyder
Judy Swett
Pam Winton

Past Commissioners

Barbara J. Smith,
   past chair
Judy Carta
Mary Louise Hemmeter

for that family rather than try to fit the family within our professional boxes.

Frequently, families don't fit in our professional boxes. Generalized understandings of families, children, and interventions—our "boxes"—help us know what to do. If X is true about this family, then this is what they need. Our boxes give us comfort because we know what to do. If we look beyond the box at the diversity reflected in each and every family, we would not have a ready-made answer or may struggle to figure out what to do next. It feels rather risky and often uncomfortable as a professional to work from uncertainty, or outside that box. But this is necessary given the uniqueness of each family. Recommended practice F6 states that practitioners provide support that is "flexible, individualized, and tailored to the family's preferences" (DEC, 2014, p. 10). EI/ECSE practitioners purposely adapt their professional tools in ways that are responsive to individual families.

All families have strengths. The risk of working outside our professional boxes is alleviated by the fact that practitioners don't have to figure out what to do by themselves. The solution lies with the family and in recognizing that all families have strengths and our role as practitioners is to "build on family strengths and capacities" (F5; DEC, 2014, p. 10). EI/ECSE practitioners take advantage of the additive effects of blending their professional knowledge and skills with the strengths of the family through reciprocal partnerships.

Families as partners. The family is a particularly powerful partner because the family knows so much more than practitioners about their hopes and dreams for their child and family, as well as the things that work well for their child and in their family. Just as interventions look different for each and every family, there are so many ways families and practitioners can "work together to create outcomes or goals, develop individualized plans, and implement practices" (F4; DEC, 2014, p. 10). EI/ECSE practitioners partner with families in ways that capitalize on individual family strengths, facilitating each family's active participation and decision making.

The ultimate outcome is for families to feel confident and competent about their abilities to support their child's development and learning. Each and every family member must come away from *every* interaction with EI/ECSE practitioners believing more in themselves than when we started. The aim of this monograph is to identify intentional ways EI/ECSE practitioners can apply the Family recommended practices—in our perspectives, words, and behaviors—that reflect this outcome within the above principles.

In This Monograph

Our intention for this monograph was to provide guidance to the EI/ECSE field, to illustrate particular ways to implement the Family recommended practices with fidelity *and* flexibility for each family. We chose articles that provide ways to think about families and our work with them as well as how we interact (what we say and do) with families and apply our professional knowledge and skills to promote family confidence and competence. We hope that as editors we represented this by assuring families also contributed to the monograph. First, as part of our call for manuscripts, we asked for articles where authentic family voices were a primary or equal contribution. Second, we asked three families who were currently supported by EI/ECSE practitioners to share their perspectives on the Family recommended practices. To facilitate their comfort, confidence, and competence in contributing, we offered families different ways to share (e.g., writing their response, participating in an interview), gave them an article (Yu, Ostrosky, Favazza, & Meyer, 2016) from Monograph No. 2 on the Environment recommended practices so they understood the context of these monographs, and asked them how best we could support them in contributing to this monograph. All three families chose to participate in an interview. We approached these conversations as an opportunity to facilitate family contributions, confident in each family's ability to decide how and what they wanted to contribute. The family and professional contributions to the monograph represent three essential themes for EI/ECSE work with families: family strengths, responsiveness to individual family diversity, and family–professional relationships.

Family Strengths

This monograph was conceptualized with an emphasis on family strengths. This theme is reflected in how the authors describe families and children (e.g., what they do versus what they don't do) and how to build relationships with families that enhance their beliefs that they can and do have the skills and knowledge to support their child's development and learning. Working from a strengths-based perspective requires appreciating and using the "capital" available in families and communities (Oakes, Jimenez-Silva, Davis, & Leon). And yet, the EI/ECSE field was not built on a strengths-based approach. Families are eligible for EI/ECSE because of their child's "deficits." This can then be perceived as something "wrong" or "missing" from what families do, most particularly when families are unsure of their strengths. As Danielle M. states in this monograph, applying the Family recommended practices "tends to become lost among the deficit language and data" and gets in the way of "building a foundation within a family."

Instead of a deficit approach, EI/ECSE practitioners can reframe or challenge "biases and beliefs widely held by . . . professionals that limit the ability to truly honor and support individual family priorities, structures, or values" (Hill, Newton, & Williams). For example, two particular strategies that work from a strengths-based perspective are to provide feedback to affirm family strengths—what they already do and what they have learned to do—to promote their child's learning (Ottley, Brown, Romano, Coogle, & Lakey) and facilitate families' use of mindful parenting when outside stresses get in the way of meeting their parenting goals (Raulston & Hansen). The monograph articles demonstrate ways to help families—with diverse backgrounds and perspectives—identify their strengths and use them to support their child.

Responsiveness to Individual Family Diversity

Families in EI/ECSE are diverse in a variety of ways, including the path to which they come to parenting such as adoption (Miller, Corr, Munger, Spence, & Santos), family learning characteristics such as parents diagnosed with intellectual disabilities (Falco, Munson, & Seifert), family career choices such as military families (Hile, Weglarz-Ward, DiPietro-Wells, Santos, & Ostrosky), and child developmental characteristics such as challenging behaviors (Joseph, Strain, & Steed). Practitioners may find it challenging to identify ways to adapt their practices with fidelity when so many diversity characteristics must be considered. The monograph contributions share ways to do just this, to connect with families and "listen, understand, and respect individual families' life circumstances, values, and beliefs . . . mindful of appreciating multiple family diversity characteristics" (Able, Amsbary, & Zheng) to then responsively partner with each and every family.

Family–Professional Relationships

When families are viewed as partners, their uniqueness and strengths become a source for solutions, enhancing the family's role as a true partner in EI/ECSE. For practitioners, this means considering the way we work to facilitate such partnerships, communicating through our words and actions that the partnership is indeed a "we" (Stephen). Instead of taking the lead in identifying potential intervention strategies, practitioners can facilitate families in taking the lead by highlighting their already existing strengths in interaction and learning, analyzing the results of their behaviors on child learning, and using videos of other families as models as opposed to professionals (Schertz & Horn).

This partnership does not end when children spend their days in the classroom (Lieberman-Betz & Chai). Instead, classroom-based practitioners find ways to support what's happening in the home. Additionally, practitioners can analyze how our words and actions can promote or impede a true partnership in program planning and implementation (Hancock, Beneke, & Cheatham). The benefits of these partnerships extend beyond individual family–professional partnerships in practice. Gavreau and Sandall share how they develop aspiring practitioners' (i.e., students) understanding of and appreciation for the lives of families of children with disabilities by partnering with families as mentors, sharing their everyday lives with students. EI/ECSE practitioners can reflect on the knowledge and strategies in this monograph to evaluate and further develop their application of the recommended practices in partnership with each and every family.

A Vision for Family Recommended Practices in the Future

This monograph demonstrates contemporary ways of using the Family recommended practices to guide one's work. These current recommended practices, and how they are implemented, will change and evolve over time as "the best available empirical evidence as well as the wisdom and experience of the field" evolves (DEC, 2014, p. 1). This progress results from both new research (i.e., empirical evidence) and critical analysis of one's intentional practice (i.e., wisdom and experience of the field). In this message, we frequently used the word *intentional*. Intentionality means working from a clearly articulated purpose and then making deliberate choices of how to work based on that purpose, or *end goal*. Two of the Family recommended practices provide those goals with regard to partnering with *all* families, namely to "promote family confidence and competence" (F5), "build on family strengths and capacities" (F5), and "support and strengthen parenting knowledge and skills" (F6).

With these goals, or *intents*, in mind, we look to the future of the Family recommended practices through the same three aspects discussed above: family strengths, responsiveness to individual family diversity, and families as partners.

Family Strengths

We envision EI/ECSE and the Family recommended practices to evolve from identifying and using family strengths to design interventions to recognizing that family strengths—what families are already doing—is the intervention itself. When "what the family does" is viewed as potential contributions to intervention design, we as practitioners, perhaps unintentionally, weigh those actions against our professional lens of what constitutes a strength and identify those strengths to the family. When "what the family does" is viewed as already-existing interventions, we seek to understand the family's lens—why they choose the approaches they do—and affirm those strengths the family uses.

This can add another level of diversity to our work. Even when families use approaches we as practitioners identify as a strength, the family may use those approaches for a different reason than we assume. And even when families use new strategies identified during intervention, they may be "complying" for the sake of their child as opposed to truly valuing the strategy. To work from this vision requires intentionally analyzing and addressing bias toward deficit-based thinking in general and in families with particular characteristics in order to trust family strengths, rationale, and choices. When this occurs, practitioners will no longer need to reframe their perspectives and will see family diversity, in all its possible forms, as inherent strengths.

Responsiveness to Individual Family Diversity

We envision EI/ECSE and the Family recommended practices to evolve from recognizing and responding to the individual diversity of each family to recognizing and responding to social and economic power structures—systemically and within each family–professional partnership—that influence families, including how families parent their children, meet their family functions, and partner with professionals. The choices families make, just as the choices we make as professionals, reflect both the individual family's values as well as their experiences within U.S. society. This requires identifying and intentionally working to build families' confidence in their place in their world, especially when families and communities do not "fit" into mainstream conceptualizations. This also requires practitioners to help individuals and their community define who they are and what they want to achieve.

Family–Professional Relationships

We envision EI/ECSE and the Family recommended practices to evolve from families and professionals partnering to design and implement individualized supports and services within professionally determined intervention structures to families and professionals co-constructing interventions and the course of interventions. This requires using the DEC Recommended Practices, in its current and future forms, as a universal design framework for how we work with each and every family. Then, the family and practitioner, together, apply those recommended practices by exploring, wondering, and questioning about child learning and development, family priorities, and how the practitioner can best support the individual family. This requires practitioners to be confident and competent in their knowledge and skills so they can flexibly apply the recommended practices while still assuring effective implementation. This also requires practitioners appreciating each partnership as a learning opportunity for themselves, as well as the family and child, which results in the co-construction of new knowledge about our practice and, subsequently, a transformation of how we practice.

We articulate this vision not to criticize where we are now but to advocate for the continued evolution of the EI/ECSE field around the way we partner with each and every family, with an appreciation for their already existing competencies. We do not know what this vision would exactly look like in practice or how to get there. We do know this vision is not solely the responsibility of practitioners but everyone involved in the EI/ECSE field. This includes (1) innovative research that contributes to redefining the Family recommended practices and how these recommended practices are effectively applied, based on new "best available empirical evidence"; (2) active examination of administrative policies and procedures that hinder effective and flexible application of the Family recommended practices and can create inequities in EI/ECSE support provision; and (3) professional development approaches for aspiring and active practitioners that promote working in increasingly sophisticated ways. At all these levels, this requires a renewed commitment to EI/ECSE work as a matter of social justice on behalf of families with young children with disabilities as well as building individual and community capacity as defined by the individuals within those communities.

Stacey Calcano, one of the family members who contributed to this monograph, clearly articulates this vision in her comments below. Stacey described how the article we provided, "'Where Are the Kids Like Me?' Classroom Environments That Help Create a Sense of Belonging" (Yu et al., 2016), increased her knowledge and how it changed her thinking about family strengths, responsiveness to individual family diversity, and family–professional relationships.

I'm going to share [the article] with a million people. . . . [It] is a perfect example of something that I know is a good idea. Of course there should be classroom materials representative of all different types of people. But, I think even myself, like other people, when you first hear that, you think of multiracial families and families with moms and families with dads. And the last light bulb goes off and you're like "Oh yeah! Of course! And kids in wheelchairs." . . . I think that one of the challenges we face is, a lot of people, their "go-to" when they think about inclusivity and diversity, particularly the word diversity, *they're really only thinking about skin color, sexual orientation, and gender. . . . It's been done in the past as well, but I feel like this generation of parents and children with disabilities are really trying to push the envelope further so that it just becomes a foregone conclusion that our kids are included in the diverse world that we all live in.*

That article, I was like "This stuff is so much better than I've ever read! . . . Of course that makes sense, these are the reasons why it's important. It's all right here in this little article." It's like, when you look at a child who has a disability, you try to keep yourself from making all of these assumptions that you wouldn't be making about this child if they didn't have a disability. To me, that seems like such a simple notion, but it's so incredibly hard for people to grasp because of societal preconceived notions about what people with disabilities are capable of doing. Or just these snap judgments that are made every single day. I know that's a hard thing to do while you're also having to think about the child's specific disability and how to help support them in their learning path. . . . That [other] article I shared (Jorgensen, 2005), it's all based on this whole idea of making the least dangerous assumption and the least dangerous assumption is to just assume that we can all do everything until we find out that we can't. Just give [families] the opportunity and let us figure out what works.

References

Division for Early Childhood. (2014). *DEC recommended practices in early intervention/early childhood special education 2014.* Retrieved from http://www.dec-sped.org/recommendedpractices

Jorgensen, C. (2005). The least dangerous assumption: A challenge to create a new paradigm. *Disability Solutions, 6*(3). Retrieved from https://www.ndss.org/Global/Least%20Dangerous%20Assumption.pdf

Yu, S., Ostrosky, M. M., Favazza, P. C., & Meyer, L. E. (2016). "Where are the kids like me?" Classroom environments that help create a sense of belonging. In T. Catalino & L. E. Meyer (Eds.), *Environment: Promoting meaningful access, participation, and inclusion* (DEC Recommended Practices Monograph Series No. 2; pp. 115–126). Washington, DC: Division for Early Childhood.

Family

Family practices refer to ongoing activities that (1) promote the active participation of families in decision-making related to their child (e.g., assessment, planning, intervention); (2) lead to the development of a service plan (e.g., a set of goals for the family and child and the services and supports to achieve those goals); or (3) support families in achieving the goals they hold for their child and the other family members.

Family practices encompass three themes:

For Your Reference

The Family recommended practices are presented here as a reference while you read these articles. We encourage you to access the entire set of DEC Recommended Practices at …

www.dec-sped.org/recommendedpractices

1. **Family-centered practices:** Practices that treat families with dignity and respect; are individualized, flexible, and responsive to each family's unique circumstances; provide family members complete and unbiased information to make informed decisions; and involve family members in acting on choices to strengthen child, parent, and family functioning.

2. **Family capacity-building practices:** Practices that include the participatory opportunities and experiences afforded to families to strengthen existing parenting knowledge and skills and promote the development of new parenting abilities that enhance parenting self-efficacy beliefs and practices.

3. **Family and professional collaboration:** Practices that build relationships between families and professionals who work together to achieve mutually agreed upon outcomes and goals that promote family competencies and support the development of the child.

We recommend the following family practices for practitioners:

F1 Practitioners build trusting and respectful partnerships with the family through interactions that are sensitive and responsive to cultural, linguistic, and socioeconomic diversity.

F2 Practitioners provide the family with up-to-date, comprehensive, and unbiased information in a way that the family can understand and use to make informed choices and decisions.

F3 Practitioners are responsive to the family's concerns, priorities, and changing life circumstances.

F4 Practitioners and the family work together to create outcomes or goals, develop individualized plans, and implement practices that address the family's priorities and concerns and the child's strengths and needs.

F5 Practitioners support family functioning, promote family confidence and competence, and strengthen family-child relationships by acting in ways that recognize and build on family strengths and capacities.

F6 Practitioners engage the family in opportunities that support and strengthen parenting knowledge and skills and parenting competence and confidence in ways that are flexible, individualized, and tailored to the family's preferences.

F7 Practitioners work with the family to identify, access, and use formal and informal resources and supports to achieve family-identified outcomes or goals.

F8 Practitioners provide the family of a young child who has or is at risk for developmental delay/disability, and who is a dual language learner, with information about the benefits of learning in multiple languages for the child's growth and development.

F9 Practitioners help families know and understand their rights.

F10 Practitioners inform families about leadership and advocacy skill-building opportunities and encourage those who are interested to participate.

1

Check Your Judgment
Reframing Techniques to Support Strengths-Based Approaches to Family-Centered Practices

CORINNE FOLEY HILL
Virginia Commonwealth University

JENNIFER RYAN NEWTON
Saint Louis University

MIRA COLE WILLIAMS
James Madison University

ALL FAMILIES LOVE THEIR CHILDREN AND WANT WHAT IS BEST FOR them. This core belief provides the basic tenet of family-centered practices. In supporting both preservice and inservice early childhood educators and practitioners, there is often the assumption that all practitioners hold this same value. Yet often during a college course or professional development experience, a participant shares, "Yes, but I know this family that honestly just doesn't care about their child. They never check backpack mail, never come to conferences, and their kid is always overly tired and late." Quickly, these perceptions (or misperceptions) challenge the strengths-based belief that families are doing the best they can within their unique circumstances and situations. How we respond will reinforce the widely held biases, will shame or diminish the courageous practitioner who gave voice to what others were thinking, or will provide opportunity for reframing.

Reframing, or "cognitive restructuring" as it is referred to in psychology (Beck, 1997), is a technique that changes the way something is expressed to communicate the idea from an alternative perspective. The participant in this scenario provides the opportunity, through guided practice and self-reflection, to reframe the belief that the stated evidence (i.e., late to school, not attending conferences) does not prove the family does not care but possibly that the family is not finding value in the experiences the school provides. This subtle but meaningful reframing shifts the responsibility from the family to the professional to take a more in-depth look at the family's priorities, values, and needs.

The Division for Early Childhood (DEC) Recommended Practices (2014) identifies family-centered practices as strategies, applications, and interactions that "treat families with dignity and respect; are individualized, flexible, and responsive to each family's unique circumstances; provide family members complete and unbiased information to make informed decisions; and involve family members in acting on choices to strengthen child, parent, and family functioning" (p. 10).

To do this well, we must tackle the challenge of biases and beliefs widely held by preservice and inservice professionals that limit the ability to truly honor and support individual family priorities, structures, or values. Reframing could provide an additional resource in the toolbox that teacher educators and professional development providers use to move practitioners forward in their implementation of the DEC Recommended Practices. Reframing could also be used to support practitioner self-reflection of their beliefs and possible biases.

We focus on four specific Family recommended practices below and provide evidence-based research related to these practices along with vignettes and reframing examples for each practice. Each vignette and reframing component draws attention to the importance of research related to family-centered practices while also providing examples to assist teacher educators, professional development providers, and practitioners in deepening their understanding of families and their ability to participate in judgment-free interactions with the families with whom they partner. *Practitioner* is used throughout to encompass preservice and inservice home-based and classroom-based early childhood service providers.

> We must tackle the challenge of biases and beliefs widely held by preservice and inservice professionals that limit the ability to truly honor and support individual family priorities, structures, or values.

F1. Practitioners build trusting and respectful partnerships with the family through interactions that are sensitive and responsive to cultural, linguistic, and socioeconomic diversity.

Practitioners frequently hold negative and preconceived biases against families whose cultural and interaction styles vary widely from their family of origin (Kim & Taylor, 2017). Perhaps without even being cognizant of these preconceptions, practitioners may compare and use their personal experiences, including child-rearing practices, as the standard of correctness. When a family deviates from these expectations, it may challenge the practitioner's capacity to "build trusting and respectful partnerships."

Scenario 1

We drove up to the trailer home, and a woman answered the door. She said she was sleeping and did not know we were coming. She did not seem ready for us, but she invited us in. We walked into a dark and smoky living area, and she turned on a light as she invited us to sit on the couch. The woman then quickly pointed to an urn on top of the mantle and told us that it was her late husband. She proceeded to talk about her family. Apparently, the child is bounced around from home to home, and she is his grandmother but has custody. I was sad to see a home full of smoke, without books or toys, and clearly not a lot of stability.

All early childhood practitioners would agree that second-hand smoke is a health hazard for young children. Additionally, they would concur that opportunities to interact with books and toys provide young children with play and early literacy experiences. Finally, practitioners recognize that children's social-emotional well-being is enhanced when they are exposed to consistent and stable environments with caregivers who support development. However, having this knowledge may cause practitioners to quickly focus on the negative aspects of this family.

Reframing 1

We drove up to the trailer home, and a woman answered the door. She appeared to be surprised that we were there for our visit but invited us in to the living room, which had electricity and was well-heated. The woman shared that her husband had recently died, and she showed us an urn that held a place of honor in the home. She shared information about her family, including that she was the child's custodial grandmother. It was clear that although the woman admitted this was not her original plan, the child appeared well-fed, clean, and attached to his grandmother.

Taking the time to listen openly helps practitioners recognize that although the child's environment could be enriched, there were many positive aspects of this family's life. Maximizing those positive aspects creates opportunity to build capacity in families through true partnership.

F3. Practitioners are responsive to the family's concerns, priorities, and changing life circumstances. Learning to balance family concerns and priorities related to their children's development with professional knowledge and expertise can be complex because it involves a set of dynamic processes (Deal, Dunst, & Trivette, 1989). The parents' goal may be for their child to learn to walk, but the physical therapist may have concerns that this may not be attainable. Another family may consistently struggle to pay the rent while the practitioner believes the family could remedy current financial difficulties by making different choices. Building capacity in practitioners to appreciate that families are entitled to their hopes and dreams for their children requires a judgment-free partnership with an emphasis on family-identified needs (Dunst & Trivette, 2009). To be truly family-centered, practitioners must recognize families have the right, without judgment, to make lifestyle choices and mistakes.

Scenario 2

When I got to the apartment, the mother told me that she was out of diapers and had only enough formula for one more bottle. I was frustrated because of the huge television and a pair of tennis shoes that I know cost more money than I could afford. It made me wonder about the choices this mother was making.

It is easy to form opinions based on observation without context. Teaching practitioners to set aside their initial assessment and probe more deeply to support the family using a coaching interaction style (Rush & Shelden, 2011) provides opportunity to modify the original opinions with fact-based context. By asking solution-focused questions, practitioners can better understand the context in which families operate.

Reframing 2

When I got to the apartment, the mother told me that she was out of diapers and had only enough formula for one more bottle. I asked the mother what her plans

were to find diapers and formula. She shared that her boyfriend managed all the finances and only gave her $20 a week. She was afraid to ask for more because he quickly became angry and threatened to kick her and the baby out.

Despite the initial impression, understanding the current life circumstances helps practitioners see that the mother's priority was her child and his immediate basic needs. Using this lens, practitioners are enabled to support families using judgment-free coaching strategies.

F5. Practitioners support family functioning, promote family confidence and competence, and strengthen family-child relationships by acting in ways that recognize and build on family strengths and capacities.
An emphasis on family-centered practices is increasing in teacher preparation programs (Hiatt-Michael, 2001; Zygmunt-Fillwalk, 2006); however, many practitioners still view themselves as the expert whose job it is to identify what is wrong with the child or determine the child's needs and then "fix the problem." Practitioners may blame families when the "fix" doesn't happen or when families behave differently than practitioners expect. Prioritizing the relationship between provider and family with the goal of increasing family members' understanding and knowledge to support their children's development requires a shift and role release for many practitioners (Childress, 2014). Practitioners must move from expert to partner because effectively collaborating with families hinges on a strengths-based approach to capacity building.

Scenario 3

Lilly will never know all of her letters. Her parents are so uninvolved. I just don't understand how a parent could not show up to any school events and then be upset with me because people are trying to help their child. I have two children, and I have always been grateful when a teacher offered help for my child.

When parents are perceived as uninvolved in early childhood settings, there is often an assumption that parents do not care or are not invested in forming a relationship with their child's school or teacher. However, by reframing, practitioners may be able to view "lack of involvement" differently and empower themselves to seek different ways to increase family engagement and focus on family strengths (Dunst & Trivette, 2009; McAllister, Green, Terry, Herman, & Mulvey, 2003) and capacities.

Reframing 3

Lilly needs some academic support, and I really want to engage her parents. I learned recently that her family is living in a homeless shelter after her dad left and her mom had to quit her evening job so someone could be with the kids at night. After talking to the mother, I learned so much about the challenges they are facing, and I asked how I could support Lilly more at school and what would be helpful for their family right now. I found out that Lilly's mom can't read but loves telling stories at home. She really wants to come to parent nights to help Lilly at home, but she has no transportation and three other small children at home. She also indicated that she feels embarrassed asking for help. Despite my initial impression, I learned that Lilly's mom is devoted and loving. I talked with her about the benefits of her storytelling and will continue to find ways to build on this strength. I am talking with my supervisor about finding ways to help transport parents to school events, and I also let Lilly's mother know that we welcome siblings and always have child care.

Engaging families in judgment-free conversations assists practitioners in recognizing family functioning styles. This open interaction lays the groundwork to appreciate family strengths, which builds the collaborative relationships between professionals and families.

F6. Practitioners engage the family in opportunities that support and strengthen parenting knowledge and skills and parenting competence and confidence in ways that are flexible, individualized, and tailored to the family's preferences. Every family's knowledge of their child's development is compounded by the multifaceted impact of culture, economics, and education. Differing beliefs, skills, values, and traditions influence family preferences and ideology (Seligman & Darling, 2007). These ideologies often shift over time and with different life circumstances. Practitioners must be flexible and willing to understand, support, and shift with the family, recognizing that readiness for capacity building must be individualized and incremental (Dunst & Trivette, 2009).

> Engaging families in judgment-free conversations assists practitioners in recognizing family functioning styles. This open interaction lays the groundwork to appreciate family strengths.

Table 1
Family-Centered Reframing

Statement	Possible reframing response
They don't try very hard	• They are content with what they have • They may need support to learn how to do new or different things
They have too many kids	• Their children bring them pleasure and joy • They value a large family
They are always looking for others to solve their problems	• They appreciate help that others can offer them • They are willing to take needed help
They are lazy	• They know how to relax • They strive to not overcommit their time
They don't want to learn English	• They value their native language • It is important to them that their children speak their native language
They look down on women	• Their culture holds men in high regard • Their family believes that men and women have specific roles and responsibilities
They spend money foolishly	• They have different priorities about material possessions that are important to them • They enjoy having fun with the money they have
They are never on time	• They are not driven by clocks and calendars • Their culture views timeliness differently than other cultures

From "Effective Partnerships: Cultural Competence," by Partnership for People With Disabilities, 2002, *Kaleidoscope: New Perspectives in Service Coordination, 3*, p. 9. Copyright 2002 by Partnership for People With Disabilities. Adapted with permission.

Scenario 4

I'm so frustrated with this family right now. They are so inflexible and insist that all of our visits happen in the afternoon because they don't like to wake up early. I think they go to parties a lot. Their son, Raphael, really needs services, but by the time I get there in the afternoon it seems like he is tired and ready for a nap, even though his mom insists that he just recently woke up. They live in a huge house, and I know they have a lot of resources, but they just prefer to focus on their adult lives rather than their child.

To "support and strengthen parenting knowledge in ways that are flexible, individualized, and tailored to the family's preferences," we must focus on respecting the varied family systems, roles, and cultural backgrounds while empowering families with knowledge and opportunities for involvement (Edwards & Da Fonte, 2012). Recognizing that families know their child and their lifestyle best reminds practitioners to honor families' priorities for their children.

Reframing 4

I'm so excited! I just learned that Raphael's dad plays in a local band that is gaining in popularity. They spend special family time going to hear the father's "gigs," which sometimes end late at night, but I love that he gets to support his dad. Now, I understand why Raphael's mother lets him sleep in later many days. Even though concerts don't happen every day, I appreciate her recognition that maintaining a consistent schedule is important for Raphael. The mother told me that meeting a little later in the afternoon would benefit them greatly. I am going to change my hours around so that I can accommodate and support this family's preferences and needs.

Families make certain parenting and lifestyle decisions based on their priorities. Practitioners are, therefore, tasked to allow themselves to be open to each family's priorities without asserting their personal biases and beliefs.

These vignettes illustrate examples of possible biases and beliefs that practitioners may hold. Reframing, an instructional tool used in supporting practitioners as they consider their personal biases related to family choices, priorities, and lifestyles, can be powerful in shifting to a strengths-based approach of family-centered practices. Used in college preparation courses as well as in professional development, participants are provided with a set of judgment-laden, biased statements about families. Facilitators then lead a discussion encouraging reframing the statements using a family-centered, strengths-based lens. After practitioners have experienced facilitated reframing, they may learn to use it as a tool for self-reflection. See Table 1 for examples of these reframed responses to common deficit statements.

While not a comprehensive list, Table 1 addresses some frequently cited biases practitioners may articulate. The vignettes illustrate common experiences that practitioners may encounter. Recognizing these biases and viewing experiences as opportunities, rather than as challenges, supports practitioners to shift their mindset. This is a first step toward effective, more meaningful, more individualized, and more rewarding partnerships on behalf of young children. Effective family-centered practices begin with the professionals. Reframing exercises can build capacity in practitioners to honor family preferences and work collaboratively toward the common goal of supporting the child's full participation in everyday routines and activities.

> Recognizing that families know their child and their lifestyle best reminds practitioners to honor families' priorities for their children.

References

Beck, A. T. (1997). The past and the future of cognitive therapy. *Journal of Psychotherapy Practice and Research, 6*, 276–284.

Childress, D. (2014, March 11). Letting it go: Role release and why it can be hard [Blog post]. Retrieved from http://veipd.org/earlyintervention/2014/03/11/letting-it-go-role-release-and-why-it-can-be-hard/

Deal, A. G., Dunst, C. J., & Trivette, C.M. (1989). A flexible and functional approach to developing Individualized Family Support Plans. *Infants and Young Children, 1*(4), 32–43.

Division for Early Childhood. (2014). *DEC recommended practices in early intervention/early childhood special education 2014.* Retrieved from http://www.dec-sped.org/recommendedpractices

Dunst, C. J., & Trivette, C. M. (2009). Capacity-building family-systems intervention practices. *Journal of Family Social Work, 12*, 119–143. doi:10.1080/10522150802713322

Edwards C. C., & Da Fonte, A. (2012). The 5-point plan: Fostering successful partnerships with families of students with disabilities. *Teaching Exceptional Children, 44*(3), 6–13. doi:10.1177/004005991204400301

Hiatt-Michael, D. (2001). *Preparing teachers to work with parents.* New York, NY: ERIC Clearinghouse on Teaching and Teacher Education. (ERIC No: ED460123)

Kim, K. J., & Taylor, L. K. (2017). Preservice teachers' self-efficacy in working with families: Can an immersive course make a difference? In J. A. Sutterby

(Ed.), *Family involvement in early education and child care* (pp. 1–22). Bingley, England: Emerald Group.

McAllister, C. L., Green, B. L., Terry, M. A., Herman, V., & Mulvey, L. (2003). Parents, practitioners, and researchers: Community-based participatory research with Early Head Start. *The American Journal of Public Health, 93,* 1672–1679.

Partnership for People With Disabilities. (2002). *Kaleidoscope: New perspectives in service coordination.* Richmond, VA: Author.

Rush, D. D., & Shelden, M. L. (2011). *The early childhood coaching handbook.* Baltimore, MD: Paul H. Brookes.

Seligman, M., & Darling, R. B. (2007). *Ordinary families, special children: A systems approach to childhood disability* (3rd ed.). New York, NY: Guilford Press.

Zygmunt-Fillwalk, E. M. (2006). The difference a course can make: Preservice teachers' perceptions of efficacy in working with families. *Journal of Early Childhood Teacher Education, 27,* 327–342. doi:10.1080/10901020600996026

It's the Professionals' Job to Inform, the Parents' Job to Decide

STACEY CALCANO
as told to Bonnie Keilty

I THINK THE [FAMILY RECOMMENDED PRACTICES] ARE GREAT. I THINK that they're all so interrelated that it almost feels like you're reading the same thing over and over again even though you aren't. That's actually a good thing.

One thing . . . I've been thinking a lot lately [is] . . . I don't think people prepare themselves enough ahead of time before walking into a family situation. I think it would be helpful so that [the professionals] bring to the table specific strategies that have been tested and known to work with a specific group of learners. The tricky thing about that is you have to be able to do it in a way that doesn't bias your position. . . . When Carter was first born, [professionals] made statements about how he may not walk until he's 3 or 4 [and said], "but for now, we'll just see how it goes." . . .

Even when we were touring preschools, one of the schools we toured . . . seemed like it would be a great school. But the director of the school was very open in saying, "He could go here for preschool, but we find that those kids do better in other schools as they get older." [At another school] . . . I'm watching their introductory video . . . [and] there's not a kid in the video with a visible disability. . . . Or, visiting classrooms that didn't have a lot of visual prompts or visual scheduling. Kids with Down syndrome are known to be very visual learners. I think that it's tricky because you can't show up at a family's house with all of these preconceived notions of what it is that child will need, but I do think that there's value in doing disability-specific research before you jump in to meet with the family.

Keep in mind that there will be a lot of families . . . who are ESL learners or for people who don't necessarily have access to computers or to the Internet or the ability to do research on their own. These [professional] connections that are made with these families could be one of the only places where these families will be receiving up-to-date, correct information and have the ability to get their hands on strategies that may work for their specific situation.

[Professionals need to be] . . . able to anticipate needs because you're also likely dealing with a parent community who doesn't even know what questions they're not asking. Like I remember even when I first started with [early intervention] for Carter. It's literally like learning a whole new language. I didn't understand. I had no idea what "OT" meant; I had never heard the term before. . . . I didn't walk out of the hospital with a book that said, "These are the things that you should be doing to help support your son in the best way that you can."

It becomes this process where parents learn a lot of this information from one another, and certainly some from our therapists. . . . For a lot of these families, the interactions they have with these educators are really going to help them figure out which way it is they should be going—or give them enough information so that they can make the decision that best serves the needs of their child. . . .

In my view, it's the role of the professional to bring to the table what the options are and to make sure that the families understand [these options]. . . . The professional, to the best of their ability, should be offering up the information and then asking the parents for their feedback on what it is that they think meets the needs of the child. Because a lot of these parents, myself included, you don't really know what's out there until you do—it takes a lot of reaching out to people, searching online, reading articles, joining Facebook groups—and then you can start to sort through the information. . . . The way that [professionals] keep it balanced is, it's the professionals' job to inform and the parents' job to decide.

Ultimately, the decision is obviously the family's. But . . . there are a lot of decisions that come up along the way that having a little [professional] guidance can be priceless to a family in trying to decipher and figure out what the right decision is. . . . It's so hard to find someone, and we've only had one person . . . who was actually able to offer up helpful information [on community resources]. . . . So, anything that [Carter] has done has been from me researching and talking to other parents and figuring out what the options are. . . . It would be helpful if, at some point, someone could be like "Have you heard about this program? They have an incredible music therapy program which could be amazing for Carter." Or just any little piece of information that I could then turn into action would be great. . . . It's not from a position of [me] not wanting to do the work. It's from a position of knowing where to start. . . . It doesn't have to be that complicated. . . . Just to lead the parent in the direction of where they can find the information that could be helpful.

I think the real tricky part of all of this is . . . [it] is extraordinarily important that [supports] be very customized and very individualized. And . . . while you're constructing how you're going to support a family, you have to keep your own personal bias at bay and not make assumptions about what the child can do . . . or what the family is capable of. . . . Just simply giving [the family] and helping [the family] manage the flow of information and opportunity. . . .

It was actually really funny because I kept just reading [the Family recommended practices] over and over again. . . . Every one of [the recommended practices] is really connected and a part of the other. They're all a part of this larger idea of being able to help families navigate a world that's very new to them to help their children learn and grow and thrive. All of those pieces are tied together and . . . [the professionals] are really the ones just helping you to simplify it. You have [for example] three different paths to choose and then you have this [professional] who can tell you about all of the obstacles or sights to see on each one of those paths so that you know ahead of time which one is going to get you to your destination quicker.

3

Feedback to Enhance Families' Competence and Confidence

Jennifer R. Ottley
Ohio University

Jennifer A. Brown
The University of Georgia

Mollie K. Romano
Florida State University

Christan Grygas Coogle
Duquesne University

Emily R. Lakey
Appalachian State University

Tania recently attended a workshop on caregiver coaching in natural environments. As an early intervention practitioner, she was excited to learn how to build her skills in providing services for infants and toddlers and their families in their home and community settings. Tania learned about the importance of not just sharing information with caregivers but using specific practices such as caregiver coaching to support family capacity building, the process in which practitioners partner with caregivers to increase their competence and confidence. The following week, Tania reviewed her notes and handouts about how practitioners and caregivers can collaborate through joint planning, observation, opportunities for practice, problem-solving, and reflection. She tried coaching each family she worked with and felt successful with some families, but she felt stuck with other families. She kept thinking about the Lamar family.

The Lamar family was receiving parenting services through child protective services, and Mr. Lamar was concerned that his son would be removed from him if he did anything wrong. Tania and Mr. Lamar had made headway in joint planning; he watched as she demonstrated use of instructional strategies, and he interacted with his son Maki throughout the session. However, when Tania tried to guide him to try a specific learning opportunity (e.g., "This would be a good time to try offering a choice."), he quickly stopped and said he had another chore to do. Tania reflected on sessions with the Lamar family, and she was feeling stuck in the "opportunities for practice" component of the coaching process. Active practice of embedded intervention strategies during the session would provide opportunities to build on Mr. Lamar's strengths and work together through feedback and reflection to identify the next steps based on the interaction. She wondered how she could support family capacity building when the active practice opportunities were limited. Tania decided that to start, she would focus on building up Mr. Lamar's confidence and competence by offering him specific feedback without any expectation of him doing something new.

Family capacity-building practices are defined as "practices that include the participatory opportunities and experiences afforded to families to strength-

en existing parenting knowledge and skills and promote the development of new parenting abilities that enhance parenting self-efficacy beliefs and practices" (Division for Early Childhood [DEC], 2014, p. 10). When practitioners expand the focus of services from imparting knowledge and skills to caregivers to also building caregivers' confidence and self-efficacy through a collaborative family-centered relationship, caregivers are equipped to flexibly use, adapt, and problem-solve the best ways to support their child's development in everyday routines and activities (Brown & Woods, 2016). In a capacity-building approach, practitioners learn about caregivers' needs and priorities as the foundation for goal setting, recognize and build on family strengths for embedded learning opportunities, and provide meaningful supports and resources to enhance child development and family functioning (see Recommended Practices F5 and F6 in DEC, 2014, p. 10).

Role of Feedback Within Coaching as a Family Capacity-Building Practice

Feedback is defined as performance-based information that comes from a person or the environment (DEC, 2015; Hattie & Timperley, 2007). Examples of feedback include the following: a practitioner sharing information with a caregiver about how well she was interacting with her child, a caregiver self-monitoring his performance using a specific strategy, and a caregiver reviewing graphed data regarding her effective use of environmental arrangement strategies. Although behaviors such as teaching a caregiver how to use a new strategy and modeling the strategy for the caregiver are important components of a capacity-building process, these behaviors would not be considered feedback because the information shared does not relate to the caregiver's performance.

Caregiver coaching is one example of a capacity-building practice that incorporates feedback (Woods, Wilcox, Friedman, & Murch, 2011). The purpose of this practice is to build caregiver capacity by increasing caregivers' competence and confidence in selecting, applying, modifying, and assessing embedded learning opportunities to increase their child's meaningful participation in the family's typical routines and activities. Throughout the coaching process, effective feedback is critical to building caregiver competence and confidence. As a practitioner draws attention to the caregiver-created learning opportunity, the caregiver is equipped to identify their action as a meaningful and intentional strategy (increasing competence) and may be encouraged by their success to use that strategy more frequently and/or to try additional strategies (increasing confidence).

For example, while singing songs, the practitioner could provide feedback by saying "that was a nice expansion; you turned his single word 'up' into a two-word phrase of 'up high.'" Feedback should connect specific cause-and-effect relationships between caregiver and child behaviors when possible. For instance, to improve a child's mobility, feedback during the routine of cleaning the kitchen table may include "when you placed your hands around her hips, that extra support helped her move from sitting to kneeling." Feedback that is honest, timely, positive, and specific; focused on observed caregiver and/or child behavior; and related to family preferences aligns with the DEC (2014) family capacity-building recommended practices. Capacity-building feedback is flexible and can be tailored to the family's preferences in a way that engages caregivers and supports family functioning by building on family capacities and strengthening caregiver-child relationships.

Providing Caregivers With Performance-Based Feedback

Feedback is delivered in a variety of ways to match the preferences, needs, and learning styles of the family as well as the available resources of both the practitioner and family. The methods of feedback that we describe below are not exhaustive, but we aim to cover the major categories of feedback that have been identified in the early childhood literature base. Research does not yet tell us which types of feedback are most effective relative to other types of feedback because few comparison studies have been conducted. However, we do know that there are a variety of evidence-based options that can support caregivers' capacity to use learning opportunities in everyday routines and activities. In the following sections, we focus on three major categories of feedback: oral, written, and video. Each type of feedback runs along a continuum of immediacy (i.e., during the interaction, later during the session, between home-visiting sessions, at the next session) and a continuum of technology use (i.e., no-tech, low-tech, high-tech). For instance, a provider could offer a family oral feedback during the context of a family routine (during the interaction, no-tech), or they could offer written feedback at the end of the session (after the interaction, low-tech). Likewise, feedback could be given with a video review a week later at the start of another home visit (next session, high-tech). Table 1 provides examples of feedback delivery across the three major categories and along the two continuums.

The subsequent sections illustrate the range of options that can be used to support caregivers by offering positive, specific feedback about how the caregiver

> Capacity-building feedback is flexible and can be tailored to the family's preferences in a way that engages caregivers and supports family functioning by building on family capacities and strengthening caregiver-child relationships.

Table 1
Examples of Feedback Delivery Options

Continuum of immediacy	Continuum of technology use		
	No tech	**Low tech**	**High tech**
During the interaction	Oral feedback during a diapering routine ("Being face to face right now helps him smile and babble with you!")	Visual cues (Providing a matrix of examples identifying opportunities to use imitation during typical routines)	Oral feedback using bug-in-ear technology while engaged in a challenging routine, such as getting child into the tub if they dislike it
After the interaction during the same session	Oral feedback at the end of a visit ("When you were changing his diaper, he was really cooing and engaged with you!")	Written notes at the end of the session (On a Post-it Note, "When you put the toy on the couch, he pulled up to get it!")	Snapping pictures or videos on a phone during the session to show caregiver-child interactions at the end of the visit
Between sessions	Oral feedback at a community outreach event ("I see you brought materials to cover the crayons to assist your child in holding them while drawing")	Meeting with the family between sessions to share data about strategy use (Meeting briefly to provide the caregiver with graphed data showing growth over the past month)	Sending e-mail or text feedback between sessions (Text: "I hope bath time has continued to go well this week! The song you sang about the fish gave him great opportunities to communicate and participate in bath time. He loved it!")
Next session	Conversing at the beginning of the next session ("Diapering with you leaning in face to face helped him talk to you last time")	Showing graphed data and written information about the caregiver's strategy use	Video feedback at the beginning of the next session (Watching the transition to bath time and pointing out strategies mom used to facilitate language)

is encouraging the child's development. Using a variety of implementation strategies may help ensure the caregiver's learning needs are addressed. Moreover, considering each of the types of feedback, along with their pros and cons, may help practitioners and caregivers determine the best match and tailor feedback delivery to each caregiver's preference.

Oral feedback. Oral feedback is verbally providing information related to caregivers' interactions with their children during their interactions or upon completion of an observation (Coogle, Ottley, Storie, Rahn, & Burt, 2017). This feedback includes recognizing a caregiver's use of practices that are known to positively impact child outcomes, such as intentionally embedding multiple learning opportunities into the activity and providing contingent reinforcement. It might also include offering corrective feedback about the caregiver's use of a strategy to further enhance the quality of their interactions with their child, such as providing feedback to offer wait time when placing items in sight but out of reach to provide a communication opportunity for the child.

The mode of oral feedback can vary. For example, oral feedback can be provided face to face during regularly scheduled home visits. In this instance, the practitioner observes the caregiver-child interaction and verbally comments on specific caregiver behaviors observed during the interaction or after the interaction. Another mode of oral feedback might include technology such as Bluetooth earpieces and cell phones or tablets to provide real-time feedback without interrupting the activities or to deliver feedback in an alternate location (i.e., bug-in-ear coaching; see Ottley, 2016). Technology-enhanced methods can be provided face to face as well as from an alternate location using platforms such as Facetime or Skype to observe live and deliver feedback.

Written feedback. Written feedback is another method to provide information regarding caregiver-child interactions (Barton, Pribble, & Chen, 2013). In this method, the practitioner observes interactions and uses text to provide feedback. Written feedback might include positive notes regarding the interactions that the practitioner observed or constructive ideas regarding the caregiver's implementation of strategies in relation to the child's goals.

Written feedback can take an array of formats from low-tech to high-tech. For example, a practitioner might take notes regarding caregiver-child interactions during a regularly scheduled home visit and share the written notes with the caregiver after the interaction. E-mail and text-messaging are other methods used to provide written feedback on caregiver-child interactions (Barton et al., 2013). Frequently, the individual providing e-mail or text feedback observes caregiver-child interactions face to face or via video and provides specific feedback to the caregiver between home-visiting sessions. This form of feedback requires few resources and can be kept by the caregiver to review and reflect upon later. When written feedback is delivered between sessions, it can serve as a prompt to encourage caregivers to embed strategies in everyday routines between visits.

Video feedback. Video feedback is a strategy in which video recordings of caregiver-child interactions are used to share observations and reflect on the interactions (Balldin, Fisher, & Wirtberg, 2016). Practitioners can video record interactions during sessions, or caregivers can share videos that they have recorded between sessions. Video feedback is used to promote caregiver competence and confidence by illustrating examples of caregivers' use of intervention strategies with their child and highlighting the connection to child outcomes. Feedback on what went well in the interaction, as well as what the caregiver could try differently next time, can support caregiver engagement and active participation in the session. For example, during video feedback, the practitioner may pause the video and ask the caregiver, "How do you think that went?" Watching oneself on video meets caregivers where they are, which strengthens the internalization and interpretation of knowledge, thereby enhancing the caregiver coaching process through observation, reflection, and problem solving.

Video feedback is used to promote caregiver competence and confidence by illustrating examples of caregivers' use of intervention strategies with their child and highlighting the connection to child outcomes.

Video feedback can be provided in person or via video conference. During intervention sessions, immediate video feedback is used in the moment. A practitioner might video record a caregiver-child interaction and then review it with the caregiver immediately following the interaction. This immediacy can be helpful in identifying additional opportunities to practice within the same session. Delayed video feedback is used when practitioners need to edit the video before showing it to the caregiver. The practitioner video records caregiver-child interactions during an intervention session and then provides video feedback using an edited video clip (Poslawsky et al., 2015), which can occur during a subsequent session or in an asynchronous manner as a component of e-mail feedback shared with caregivers between sessions. With ever-increasing advances in technology, video feedback is a flexible tool that can easily be individualized to provide feedback within families' everyday routines and activities.

After a session, Tania tells Mr. Lamar that one of her main roles is to help him see how he is supporting Maki to move and communicate. She says, "One of my jobs is to point out when you are using a strategy to help Maki develop, because sometimes parents don't recognize all that they are doing! Would you prefer that I jot down some notes or say my thoughts out loud?" Mr. Lamar says he likes notes because it takes him longer to listen and process what Tania says while he is still focused on Maki. He asks Tania if they could try the notes and see how it goes. He asks her to text him the notes so he does not misplace them.

Benefits of Using Feedback With Caregivers

Benefits associated with oral, written, and video feedback include increased (a) caregiver self-efficacy (e.g., feelings of competence, confidence that they are using strategies correctly; Ottley, Coogle, & Rahn, 2015) and (b) quantity and quality of caregivers' use of targeted recommended practices (e.g., positive caregiver-child interactions, embedding learning opportunities into typical routines; Balldin et al., 2016; Brown & Woods, 2016). Performance-based feedback also promotes growth in children's behaviors identified through individualized plans and targeted through intervention sessions (Coogle et al., 2017; Poslawsky et al., 2015).

After their conversation, Tania offered some written feedback (the mode that Mr. Lamar preferred). As she observed Mr. Lamar and Maki at the playground, she wrote positive notes about their mutual engagement in the interaction. "When you were chasing and catching each other, you were providing opportunities for Maki to work toward his movement outcomes by running around. I can see that his coordination is improving and activities like this will continue to support that." Tania also noticed occasions where Maki would gaze at the slide, although they never used it during play. Tania continued in her note, "Maki seems to be interested in the slide. By helping him climb up the stairs, he can develop his mobility in another highly motivating activity, because he will be rewarded with the slide after he climbs the stairs." As Tania was leaving, she told Mr. Lamar that she enjoyed seeing Maki run and play with him, texted him the written feedback, and stated

For feedback to be most effective, practitioners should flexibly deliver it in a manner that is respectful to caregivers' preferences.

that she looked forward to their next session.

The next week she again met the Lamar family at the playground. She observed Mr. Lamar providing Maki with verbal prompts and encouragement to climb. "Lift your foot . . . this is the top step . . . now your left foot . . . you can do it." She then observed Maki sit down and wiggle himself forward until he slid down the slide. Maki smiled as he looked at Mr. Lamar and said "slide." Mr. Lamar carried Maki to the stairs and placed him on the second from the top step and again provided encouragement as Maki climbed two stairs.

Tania wrote about her observation. "Mr. Lamar, Maki was really climbing today, and you helped him do it by giving him just a bit of help. You gave him a fun chance to practice climbing using an activity you both enjoy, and he did it! He even let you know that he wanted to slide again. Did you notice that he said 'slide'? That would be a good chance for you to model a two-word phrase like 'go slide.' I also noticed that you gave him another chance to try climbing by starting again from the second step. This is excellent because it gives him a little more work to do! Another way to strengthen his movement skills would be to walk with him around the slide and then pick him up at the base of the steps." Embedded in the message was a picture she took of Mr. Lamar helping Maki climb the

slide as a way to help him remember those moments. Tania sent the text message feeling excited about the possibilities that feedback provides for active practice opportunities for families.

The Importance of Individualizing the Format of Feedback for Caregivers

When providing feedback, a number of challenges can arise, but each can be minimized through joint planning and tailoring feedback to each family. For feedback to be most effective, practitioners should flexibly deliver it in a manner that is respectful to caregivers' preferences. This can be accomplished by asking open-ended questions regarding caregivers' priorities and concerns for their child's development and then referencing types of feedback that could be used to support caregivers in creating learning opportunities for their child to practice family-identified skills. By delivering feedback that is aligned with target outcomes, practitioners act in a manner that is responsive to caregivers' priorities and caregivers actively participate in the decision-making process, which can promote self-efficacious parenting beliefs and a commitment to creating meaningful learning opportunities for the child (de la Rie, van Steensel, & van Gelderen, 2017). Another way that practitioners can individualize feedback is in the dosage provided to caregivers. Although the research literature does not provide a clear intensity of feedback necessary to promote sustained change in caregiver and child outcomes, some research suggests that the dose (mean rate of feedback delivered per session), dose frequency (how often feedback is provided), dose duration (the total time over which feedback is provided), and dose form (how feedback is delivered) are each important considerations that may have differential effects on children's outcomes (Warren, Fey, & Yoder, 2007).

Whereas some may think dose frequency is limited to the number of intervention sessions outlined in a child's individualized plan, practitioners may only be limited by their ingenuity. If a child received one hour of early intervention services every other week, a practitioner could combine feedback mechanisms so that the dose frequency could be greater. For example, the practitioner could video record an interaction and provide oral feedback after the interaction and then also send a video clip with accompanying written feedback using e-mail the next week to double the "dose." In this manner, caregivers receive feedback in diverse forms and at a greater frequency than if feedback were only provided during the family's scheduled early intervention sessions. Practitioners and caregivers can work together to set goals for the frequency with which caregivers should aim to use embedded learning opportunities (Casey & McWilliam, 2011). This implementation goal should be flexibly created based on data regarding the caregiver's current level of performance and the strengths and needs of the child. By monitoring caregivers' use of strategies and assessing children's outcomes, practitioners can evaluate whether the intensity of feedback delivered is sufficient for building caregivers' capacity to use and generalize practices.

Final Thoughts Regarding Feedback

Feedback can be a flexible mechanism to provide individualized information to caregivers regarding their performance in interacting with their child. Feedback builds on a family's strengths. It can be tailored to caregivers' preferences and aligned with their priorities and concerns for their child. Feedback can strengthen caregivers' knowledge, which in turn can promote their competence and confidence to use recommended practices. Yet, capacity building is more than caregivers learning to use a skill, it is about consistently using it across the typical routines of the family's natural environment. Thus, practitioners should evaluate whether the feedback they provide within the broader caregiver coaching model is sufficient to support sustained and generalized use of embedded learning opportunities. By partnering with families, practitioners can provide individualized feedback that actively engages caregivers, meets their learning needs, strengthens their capacity, and ultimately enhances children's outcomes.

References

Balldin, S., Fisher, P. A., & Wirtberg, I. (2016). Video feedback intervention with children: A systematic review. *Research on Social Work Practice*. Advance online publication. doi:10.1177/1049731516671809

Barton, E. E., Pribble, L., & Chen, C.-I. (2013). The use of e-mail to deliver performance-based feedback to early childhood practitioners. *Journal of Early Intervention, 35*, 270–297. doi:10.1177/1053815114544543

Brown, J. A., & Woods, J. J. (2016). Parent-implemented communication intervention: Sequential analysis of triadic relationships. *Topics in Early Childhood Special Education, 36*, 115–124. doi:10.1177/0271121416628200

Casey, A. M., & McWilliam, R. A. (2011). The characteristics and effectiveness of feedback interventions applied in early childhood settings. *Topics in Early Childhood Special Education, 31*, 68–77. doi:10.1177/0271121410368141

Coogle, C. G., Ottley, J. R., Storie, S., Rahn, N. L., & Burt, A. K. (2017). eCoaching to enhance educator practice and child outcomes. *Infants and Young Children, 30*, 58–75. doi:10.1097/IYC.0000000000000082

de la Rie, S., van Steensel, R. C. M., & van Gelderen, A. J. S. (2017). Implementation quality of family literacy programmes: A review of literature. *Review of Education, 5*, 91–118. doi:10.1002/rev3.3081

Division for Early Childhood. (2014). *DEC recommended practices in early intervention/early childhood special education 2014*. Retrieved from http://www.dec-sped.org/recommendedpractices

Division for Early Childhood. (2015). *DEC recommended practices glossary*. Retrieved from http://www.dec-sped.org/recommendedpractices

Hattie, J., & Timperley, H. (2007). The power of feedback. *Review of Educational Research, 77*, 81–112. doi:10.3102/003465430298487

Ottley, J. R. (2016). Real-time coaching with bug-in-ear technology: A practical approach to support families in their child's development. *Young Exceptional Children, 19*(3), 32–46. doi:10.1177/1096250615576806

Ottley, J. R., Coogle, C. G., & Rahn, N. L. (2015). The social validity of bug-in-ear coaching: Findings from two studies implemented in inclusive early childhood environments. *Journal of Early Childhood Teacher Education, 36*, 342–361. doi:10.1080/10901027.2015.1100146

Poslawsky, I. E., Naber, F. B. A., Bakermans-Kranenburg, M. J., van Daalen, E., van Engeland, H., & van IJzendoorn, M. H. (2015). Video-feedback Intervention to promote Positive Parenting adapted to Autism (VIPP-AUTI): A randomized controlled trial. *Autism, 19*, 588–603. doi:10.1177/1362361314537124

Warren, S. F., Fey, M. E., & Yoder, P. J. (2007). Differential treatment intensity research: A missing link to creating optimally effective communication interventions. *Mental Retardation and Developmental Disabilities Research Reviews, 13*, 70–77. doi:10.1002/mrdd.20139

Woods, J. J., Wilcox, M. J., Friedman, M., & Murch, T. (2011). Collaborative consultation in natural environments: Strategies to enhance family-centered supports and services. *Language, Speech, and Hearing Services in Schools, 42*, 379–392. doi:10.1044/0161-1461(2011/10-0016)

4

Addressing DEC's Family Recommended Practices
Community Cultural Wealth Framework

Wendy Peia Oakes
Margarita Jimenez-Silva
Arizona State University

Lauren Marie Davis
Veronica Leon
Phoenix, Arizona

THE STATED PURPOSE OF THE DIVISION FOR EARLY CHILDHOOD (DEC) Recommended Practices (2014) is to "provide guidance to practitioners and families about the most effective ways to improve the learning outcomes and promote the development of young children, birth through age 5, who have or are at-risk for developmental delays or disabilities" (p. 3). It is implied in the purpose statement that practitioners and families are equal partners in the process of supporting the child's development. In introducing the Family recommended practices, DEC makes explicit the expectation that practitioners will "treat families with dignity and respect" and that the practices will "build relationships between families and professionals who work together" to the benefit of the child (p. 10).

While a number of courses in our early childhood special education teacher preparation program discuss the concept of working with families, we found that few class discussions, readings, or assignments addressed in detail the importance of approaching our work with families from a perspective that emphasizes reciprocity among the various key stakeholders in the education of our youngest learners. This is not uncommon. In a study of teacher education programs across the country, Broussard (2000) reported the presence of family-friendly language and family content in preservice teacher education curricula as weak, although improved since the early 1990s, when such language was minimal. Furthermore, Broussard found that teachers and administrators reported a lack of preparation in "concrete knowledge, skills, and positive attitudes about parent involvement" (p. 41). More recently, Vaughns (2016) stated that educators continue to report feeling unprepared to work with families, especially with linguistically, culturally, and socioeconomically diverse families. Partnerships with families take effort, skills, knowledge, dispositions, and time (Knight-McKenna & Hollingsworth, 2016).

Family engagement and developing a reciprocal relationship is especially critical when working with young culturally and linguistically diverse (CLD) children with delays and disabilities. These families often face challenges with language barriers, navigating the educational system, sharing information in accessible ways, and appropriateness of assessment tools and practices for parents to be part of the assessment process (Banerjee & Guiberson, 2012). While developing reciprocal relationships may present challenges for early childhood special educators, 21st century teachers are expected to have the skills and dispositions for building such partnerships with the diverse families they will serve (Knight-McKenna & Hollingsworth, 2016).

Early childhood classrooms across the country are becoming more diverse while teachers remain primarily White (82%; U.S. Department of Education, 2016). In 2011, approximately 27% of kindergarteners were from immigrant families (Sullivan, Houri, & Sadeh, 2016). National data show an increasing trend of English learners (EL) in public school. In 2014, 17.4% of kindergarteners were ELs while ELs made up a total of 9.3% of all students PreK to 12th grade (Kena et al., 2016). The primary home language for ELs was Spanish (76.5% of all ELs). During this time, schools also served 13% of students with disabilities (Kena et al., 2016). Early childhood special education (ECSE) teacher preparation programs are charged with readying teachers with culturally responsive practices for children who are CLD with delays and disabilities and in recruiting a diverse group of teacher candidates.

Teacher Preparation for Early Childhood Special Educators

One of the largest teacher preparation programs in the Southwestern United States has accepted this charge by preparing approximately 100 early childhood special educators each year who are well-qualified teachers for children who are CLD with delays and disabilities attending high-need school districts and their families. Selected teacher candidates participate in the ECSE Scholars program, funded by the U.S. Department of Education's Office of Special Education Programs (OSEP). As of May 2017, the program has graduated 39 ECSE scholars with dual certification in early childhood and special education. One priority is to recruit diverse teacher candidates to reflect the student populations they are serving (Kidd, Sánchez, & Thorp, 2008). To date, more than 40% of the scholars represent culturally and/or linguistically diverse groups or have disabilities. As part of the program, ECSE scholars engage in coursework, professional learning and leadership opportunities, and experiences to develop their intercultural competence and prepare them to meet the educational needs of the state's young children who are CLD with delays and disabilities.

As part of this work, courses were revised to offer ECSE teacher candidates additional experiences with children's families in their communities, recognizing that family engagement needs particular intentionality when working with CLD children with delays and disabilities (Howes, 2010). Improvements and experiences were the result of ECSE scholars' feedback and recommendations, a review

Family engagement and developing a reciprocal relationship is especially critical when working with young culturally and linguistically diverse children with delays and disabilities.

of program syllabi, faculty planning, and additional funding through a private foundation. Teacher candidates participating in the ECSE scholars program prepare to work with families in culturally respectful and responsive ways, drawing on the strengths of families using a funds of knowledge approach (Moll, Amanti, Neff, & Gonzalez, 1992) and a community cultural wealth framework (Yosso, 2005).

A Community Cultural Wealth Perspective for Working With Families

A number of approaches have been used historically when addressing the physical, social, cognitive, communicative, and adaptive needs of our youngest culturally and linguistically diverse (CLD) children. Deficit approaches have prevailed in our educational system as CLD children's backgrounds and children with disabilities were seen to have deficiencies that needed to be overcome (Kozleski & Huber, 2010; Lee, 2007).

The goal of deficit approaches was to "eradicate the linguistic, literate, and cultural practices many students of color brought from their homes and communities and to replace them with what were viewed as superior practices" (Paris, 2012, p. 93). During the 1970s and 1980s, a differences approach gained momentum and the backgrounds of CLD children were discussed as being different but equal to the ways "demanded and legitimized in school teaching and learning" (Paris, 2012, p. 94). Differences approaches evolved into resource pedagogies in the 1990s and

the most well-known of these is the funds of knowledge framework put forth by Moll and González (1994). The funds of knowledge framework recognized the "historically accumulated and culturally developed bodies of knowledge and skills" (Moll & González, 1994, p. 443) each family possesses and called teachers to tap into that knowledge when working with children. The concepts of culturally relevant pedagogy (Ladson-Billings, 1995) and culturally responsive pedagogy (Gay, 2010) then called on us, as educators, to consider CLD children's heritage and traditional practices when working in the classroom.

Yosso (2005) expanded on these concepts by introducing us to a framework that presents community cultural wealth as "an array of knowledge, skills, abilities, and contacts possessed and utilized by Communities of Color" (p. 77) to navigate systems such as our educational settings. The community cultural wealth framework identifies six types of capital that families possess: aspirational, linguistic, familial, social, navigational, and resistant (Yosso, 2005). Aspirational capital refers to the ability to maintain hopes for the future despite any barriers that may be real or perceived. Linguistic capital encompasses the social skills and intellect acquired through communication experiences in more than one language, acknowledging that many CLD children arrive at school with multiple language and communication skills.

Familial capital refers to the cultural knowledge nurtured among family members and carries a "sense of community history, memory, and cultural intuition" (Yosso, 2005, p. 79). Social capital includes networks of community resources and people that provide support through various institutions in society. Navigational capital, recognizing many institutions are not created with CLD communities in mind, refers to skills required to make one's way through social institutions. The final form is resistant capital, which refers to the skills and knowledges "fostered through oppositional behavior that challenges inequality" (Yosso, 2005, p. 80).

Honoring our grant commitment to prepare ECSE scholars to work reciprocally with families of CLD children with delays and disabilities, we adopted

Yosso's (2005) community cultural wealth framework. We engaged scholars in various professional learning opportunities in which we discussed how we have approached our work with families of CLD children with disabilites using this framework, which aligns with the Family recommended practices. Examples of these professional learning opportunities included expert panel discussions, a book study, Council for Exceptional Children (CEC) convention attendance and focus groups, and discussion groups with faculty mentors. Four panel discussions were held during the academic year on (a) working with families and children who are in foster care, (b) working with related service providers and families to meet the comprehensive needs of children and families, (c) developing individual family service plans (IFSP) with families and transitioning families and children to individualized education plans (IEP), and (d) working with CLD children with delays and disabilities and their families. Three panel members participated in each topic representing school professionals, agency professionals, and parents.

In another professional learning experience, scholars participated in a book study, reading Klingner and Eppolito's 2014 book, *English Language Learners: Differentiating Between Language Acquisition and Learning Disabilities.* The book study engaged scholars in interactive games and round-table discussions on topics related to the text. The book study was led by scholars with topics for discussion generated by faculty mentors and scholars. Scholars began the discussion session with a game on some of the key learning points, then discussed topics submitted in advance and those that developed organically during the discussion. Scholars applied the topics to their experiences as new teachers and teacher candidates.

Scholars attended CEC conventions in the final year of their preparation program, with some continuing to attend as they began their careers. Convention sessions on families were the focus of their 2016 convention experience. Scholars attended sessions related to working with families, and at the end of the convention, they met with faculty mentors for a focus group on their experiences and how the experiences would inform their work with families.

Scholars also met formally and informally with faculty mentors to reflect on their experiences in the ECSE preparation program. Reflections were used by faculty to revise course syllabi. Course improvements included assignment revisions with additional experiences in talking with families about their child's progress, learning needs, and their families' priorities. Program improvements resulted in a greater focus on reciprocal relationships between families and practitioners.

We invited scholars to think about how they could apply this framework when working with families and share with their classmates and colleagues specific examples from their classrooms. As scholars have graduated and are now in their own classrooms, they continue to share success stories using the language of community wealth along with the language of the Family recommended practices (DEC, 2014). They were excited to discuss their successes and have presented their experiences in various general and special education forums. In the next section, we share the voices of two of our ECSE scholar graduates.

Voices From the Field

Lauren Davis, preschool special education teacher. *Parents are a child's first teacher and a teacher's greatest resource.* I am a first-year teacher at a Title I school. I teach 22 preschool children with disabilities in two classes. ELs comprise 31.82% of my students, 81.82% are CLD, and all have an IEP. Through my experiences as an ECSE scholar, my student teaching, and my coursework, I have learned skills for recognizing and using different kinds of wealth in my practice with students' families and their community.

These ways of thinking are part of my daily practice in my classroom and on our early childhood campus. One example is my opportunity to visit each child's home. Teachers visit homes and communities in which our students live. We take this time to develop a reciprocal relationship with the children's families to support each other on behalf of the child. On home visits, we are intentional in learning about families' priorities for their children. We then create goals that parents feel are important for their child to achieve; these may be in addition to the IEP goals already in place. Examples of goals identified by families were writing skills such as tracing, developing phonemic awareness, or learning how to play and get along with other children in the classroom. This practice is informed by our understanding of familial and aspirational wealth (Yosso, 2005) and Family recommended practices F1, F3, and F4 (see Table 1). We are taking into consideration not only the family's hopes and dreams for their child but also what families find important for their children.

> As scholars have graduated and are now in their own classrooms, they continue to share success stories using the language of community wealth along with the language of the Family recommended practices.

Table 1
DEC Recommended Practices and the Community Cultural Wealth Model

DEC Recommended Family Practices	Types of Capital					
	Aspirational	Linguistic	Familial	Social	Navigational	Resistant
F1 Practitioners build trusting and respectful partnerships with the family through interactions that are sensitive and responsive to cultural, linguistic, and socioeconomic diversity.		X	X	X		X
F2 Practitioners provide the family with up-to-date, comprehensive, and unbiased information in a way that they can understand and use to make informed choices and decisions.	X		X	X	X	X
F3 Practitioners are responsive to the family's concerns, priorities, and changing life circumstances.	X		X	X		X
F4 Practitioners and the family work together to create outcomes or goals, develop individualized plans, and implement practices that address the family's priorities and concerns and the child's strengths and needs.	X		X	X	X	
F5 Practitioners support family functioning, promote family confidence and competence, and strengthen family-child relationships by acting in ways that recognize and build on family strengths and capacities.	X	X	X	X		
F6 Practitioners engage the family in opportunities that support and strengthen parenting knowledge and skills and parenting competence and confidence in ways that are flexible, individualized, and tailored to the family's preferences.				X	X	X
F7 Practitioners work with the family to identify, access, and use formal and informal resources and supports to achieve family-oriented outcomes and goals.	X	X	X	X	X	X
F8 Practitioners provide family of a young child who has or is at risk for developmental delay/disability, and who is a dual language learner, with information about the benefits of learning in multiple languages for the child's growth and development.		X	X	X		
F9 Practitioners help families know and understand their rights.					X	X
F10 Practitioners inform families about leadership and advocacy skill-building opportunities and encourage those who are interested to participate.	X		X	X	X	X

During the visits, I share data to show their child's progress, focusing on strengths and individual goals and Teaching Strategies Gold (Heroman, Burts, Berke, & Bickart, 2010), our observation-based preschool assessment system, and data collected through detailed anecdotal records. Sharing data with parents accounts for navigational wealth and for informing parents of their child's most current progress so they can make decisions for their child (F2).

Home visits are a time when we learn about families, ask how we can support them, and share available resources. We focus on families' linguistic wealth and the multiple community resources. In one experience, a family asked for help with their child's tantrums and refusal to wear long sleeves. School therapists, parents, and I worked together on a deescalation plan where parents offered the child choices for getting dressed in the morning (Colvin & Scott, 2015; Palmer et al., 2013). This slight change made transitions easier for the child and family.

During each visit, I am able to work with families to address individual needs. A recent example is when a family who has two children transitioning to kindergarten asked for information on different programs offered by the district. To meet the family's need, I researched district programs, put some information together for the family, and secured permission to tour a program that is available to both children. With this information, the family will be able to advocate effectively for their children based on their individual strengths and needs. I was able to build social and resistant wealth with this parent, and because of this, we have a strong working relationship, and we are both seeing growth in her child who is in my class.

Veronica Leon, preschool special education teacher. *My role in the classroom is to teach the way each of my students learn.* I am in my third year of teaching preschool special education in South Phoenix. Our preschool serves more than 120 children ages 3 to 5 with a wide range of cognitive, social, and physical abilities. There is a strong emphasis on parent and family involvement across the program. We offer monthly field trips at a discounted rate and host events on campus. The campus is family-centered, and we engage our families as partners in various ways, including hosting guest speakers who draw on families' community cultural wealth as well as develop their navigational knowledge of how to access various services (F2 and F7).

One of my goals is to bring children's culture into the classroom by inviting families to join in the learning. I believe it is critical to build on families' strengths and capacities. I know that it is important to build trusting and respectful partnerships with families through interactions that are sensitive and responsive to cultural, linguistic, and socioeconomic diversity (F1).

One way I have engaged families is by inviting them to share during our weekly show and tell. Children bring an item from home they would like to share with their classmates. This item could be related to the monthly theme or color but is something of special meaning to them. Families are also invited to participate in a cultural show and tell where they share an item, story, song, or game with the class that explains something about their culture or family heritage. One year, a child's mother taught our students how to play Loteria, also known as Mexican bingo. She explained the origin of the game, talked about the illustrations on the cards, and showed them how to play. Children played the game

> Home visits are a time when we learn about families, ask how we can support them, and share available resources. We focus on families' linguistic wealth and the multiple community resources.

with her as she called out different illustrations. All children were engaged and learned about a special tradition of one of their peers.

Next Steps: ECSE Teachers as Advocates for Young Children Who Are CLD With Delays and Disabilities

As advocates of children and families using a framework honoring the cultural wealth of families, we continue to improve our program for ECSE scholars and all teacher candidates as they develop the knowledge, dispositions, and skills to meaningfully partner with families. We are engaging with faculty to expand on readings, assignments, and applied projects to better prepare our teachers. We will continue to offer professional learning for ECSE scholars on strategies for engaging with families in ways that are "sensitive and responsive to cultural, linguistic, and socioeconomic diversity" (F1). Experiences include those discussed previously, such as panels of guest speakers who talk about work with parents and community resources, scholar-led book studies (Klingner & Eppolito, 2014), small group faculty discussions of effective practices, and attendance at professional conferences (e.g., CEC convention and expo, DEC conference), to name a few. By addressing the Family recommended practices (DEC, 2014) from a community cultural wealth framework, we are honoring the goal of partnering with families in respectful and dignified ways that allow for mutual learning and building authentic relationships that will ultimately benefit the children we serve.

Note

The contents of this paper were developed under a grant from the U.S. Department of Education, No. H325K130412. However, the contents do not necessarily represent policies of the U.S. Department of Education and should not be assumed to be endorsed by the federal government or the project officer, Traci Dickson.

References

Banerjee, R., & Guiberson, M. (2012). Evaluating young children from culturally and linguistically diverse backgrounds for special education services. *Young Exceptional Children, 15*(1), 33–45. doi:10.1177/1096250611435368

Broussard, C. A. (2000). Preparing teachers to work with families: A national survey of teacher education programs. *Equity & Excellence in Education, 33*(2), 41–49. doi:10.1080/1066568000330207

Colvin, G., & Scott, T. M. (2015). *Managing the cycle of acting-out behavior in the classroom* (2nd ed.). Thousand Oaks, CA: Corwin Press.

Division for Early Childhood (2014). *DEC recommended practices in early intervention/early childhood special education 2014.* Retrieved from http://www.dec-sped.org/dec-recommended-practices

Gay, G. (2010). *Culturally responsive teaching: Theory, research, and practice* (2nd ed). New York: NY. Teachers College.

Heroman, C., Burts, D. C., Berke, K., & Bickart, T. S. (2010). *Teaching strategies gold objectives for development and learning.* Washington, DC: Teaching Strategies.

Howes, C. (2010). *Culture and child development in early childhood programs: Practices for quality education and care.* New York, NY: Teachers College Press.

Kena, G., Hussar, W., McFarland, J., de Brey, C., Musu-Gillette, L., Wang, X., . . . Dunlop Velez, E. (2016). *The condition of education 2016* (NCES 2016-144). Washington, DC: U.S. Department of Education, National Center for Education Statistics.

Kidd, J. K., Sánchez, S. Y., & Thorp, E. K. (2008). Defining moments: Developing culturally responsive dispositions and teaching practices in early childhood preservice teachers. *Teaching and Teacher Education, 24,* 316–329. doi:10.1016/j.tate.2007.06.003

Klingner, J., & Eppolito, A. (2014). *English language learners: Differentiating between language acquisition and learning disabilities.* Arlington, VA: Council for Exceptional Children.

Knight-McKenna, M., & Hollingsworth, H. L. (2016). Fostering family-teacher partnerships: Principles in practice. *Childhood Education, 92,* 383–390. doi:10.1080/00094056.2016.1226113

Kozleski, E. B., & Huber, J. J. (2010). Systemic change for RTI: Key shifts for practice. *Theory Into Practice, 49,* 258–264. doi:10.1080/00405841.2010.510696

Ladson-Billings, G. (1995). But that's just good teaching! The case of culturally relevant pedagogy. *Theory Into Practice, 34,* 159–165. doi:10.1080/00405849509543675

Lee, C. D. (2007). *Culture, literacy, and learning; Taking bloom in the midst of the whirlwind.* New York, NY: Teachers College Press.

Moll, L. C., Amanti, C., Neff, D., & Gonzalez, N. (1992). Funds of knowledge for teaching: Using a qualitative approach to connect homes and classrooms. *Theory Into Practice, 31,* 132–141. doi:10.1080/00405849209543534

Moll, L. C., & González, N. (1994). Lessons from research with language-minority children. *Journal of Reading Behavior, 26,* 439–456. doi:10.1080/10862969409547862

Palmer, S. B., Summers, J. A., Brotherson, M. J., Erwin, E. J., Maude, S. P., Stroup-Rentier, V., . . . Haines, S. J. (2013). Foundations for self-determination in early childhood: An inclusive model for children with disabilities. *Topics in Early Childhood Special Education, 33,* 38–47. doi:10.1177/0271121412445288

Paris, D. (2012). Culturally sustaining pedagogy: A needed change in stance, terminology, and practice. *Educational Researcher, 41,* 93–97. doi:10.3102/0013189X12441244

Sullivan, A. L., Houri, A., & Sadeh, S. (2016). Demography and early academic skills of students from immigrant families: The kindergarten class of 2011. *School Psychology Quarterly, 31,* 149–162. doi:10.1037/spq0000137

U.S. Department of Education. (2016, July). *The state of racial diversity in the educator workforce.* Washington, DC: Author.

Vaughns, A. (2016). Focus on family: A double-edged sword: Preparing preservice teachers to work with diverse families through community-based learning, *Childhood Education, 92,* 419–422. doi:10.1080/00094056.2016.12 26119

Yosso, T. J. (2005). Whose culture has capital? A critical race theory discussion of community cultural wealth. *Race, Ethnicity and Education, 8,* 69–91. doi:10.1080/1361332052000341006

5

Application of DEC Family-Centered Practices
Where the Rubber Meets the Road

Harriet Able
Jessica Amsbary
Shuting Zheng
University of North Carolina at Chapel Hill

THERE ARE A WIDE RANGE OF DIVERSITY CHARACTERISTICS OF CHILdren and families served in early intervention programs. Given the diverse demographics of the 21st century family, early childhood interventionists need to embrace a broader definition of diversity to include individual differences in culture, language, ability, and learning styles of young children with an added focus on families with diverse structures and socioeconomic levels. This translates into services reflecting a broad-based, antibiased orientation to assessment and intervention that foster inclusion and interaction among children of differing ethnicities, languages, backgrounds, and abilities in a climate of mutual respect and appreciation of difference referred to as "cultural democracy" (Hoffman-Kipp, 2003). Further, to realize the full intent of the Division for Early Childhood (DEC) Recommended Practices (2014), family-centered practitioners need to be (a) socioculturally and linguistically responsive, (b) avid and informed consumers of evidence-based practice research, and (c) leaders and advocates for children and families focusing on family strengths and capacity building.

In addition to the DEC Recommended Practices (2014), a landmark policy statement from the U.S. Departments of Health and Human Services and Education (2016) regarding family engagement recommends *essential* partnerships with families by nurturing positive relationships and supporting families focusing on family wellness. This policy statement also emphasizes the critical role of responsive practitioners who honor and respect families' cultural and linguistic backgrounds and unique experiences in supporting their young children's development. In sum, we, as early childhood interventionists, need to respect and embrace families' unique backgrounds and circumstances through building close partnerships with families.

Table 1
Practice Checklist for Engaging in Sensitive, Respectful, and Responsive Interactions

☐	Be aware of your values and preferences and regularly reflect with colleagues to guard against biases.
☐	Recognize that there are no "cookie cutter" families—all families are individual and unique.
☐	Accept families where they are based on individual family circumstances and not where you may think the family should be.
☐	Establish partnerships with families by being responsive and open-minded.
☐	Spend time getting to know the family and understanding children's strengths and needs from the family's perspective.
☐	Ask questions such as: What is your child really good at? What are her/his greatest strengths? What does he/she like to do? What can we do to help your child succeed? How does your child learn best? What does he/she like about school? What do you want your child to be like when he/she is 3 or goes to first grade? Do you have any family traditions or routines that we need to be aware of when working with your child?
☐	Meet with families in their homes or community settings when and where they feel most comfortable.
☐	Allow time for families to listen and understand the information concerning their children and services.
☐	Provide opportunities for follow up so families can continue to ask questions and seek information as needed.

However, despite the multiple efforts to prepare early childhood professionals to become culturally responsive practitioners, there are service delivery gaps, which cause us not to realize the full intent of family-centered services (Dunst, 2002). In this article, we will highlight family-centered practice dilemmas described by early intervention practitioners. These dilemmas are taken from sessions referred to as Reconnect and Recharge (R&R), which are conducted to support the induction of graduates of an early childhood intervention master's degree program in the Southeastern United States. Graduates participate in R&R sessions in which they share their practice dilemmas related to the recommended practices in their work settings. An overarching theme across dilemmas is the practitioners' descriptions of "where the rubber meets the road" and how they apply the DEC Recommended Practices (2014) when delivering family-centered services. For example, here's how one participant described a practice dilemma:

> I have two families now that are in a homeless shelter. Both have children who get multiple services. But I can't help but think: "Where did the SSI check go? Why were they evicted if both parents were supposedly working full time because they supposedly can't ever come to school meetings?" And, it is hard not to be a little resentful. *But I have to just back off and accept them for who they are.*

This practitioner clearly understands that to fully realize family-centered services, she/he needs to fully accept and respect families and their life circumstances. This approach implies responsive and respectful partnerships leading to family capacity-building practices. In this paper, we describe strategies to assist practitioners in resolving their practice dilemmas by using the DEC Recommended Practices as guidance for problem solving and practice.

Table 2
Practice Checklist for Strengthening Family Knowledge, Skills, and Competence

	Accept families where they are on the engagement continuum and begin capacity building from there.
	Focus on helping families become informed consumers and decision-makers for their children by collaborating with cultural guides and family mentors as needed.
	Provide families with necessary information related to their child's disability.
	Provide families with knowledge and skills in using evidence-based practices, if applicable.
	Provide families information on available supports and resources.
	Provide ongoing coaching (including supports, feedback, and/or suggestions) that aligns with families' needs, priorities, and goals.
	Provide feedback and encourage family self-reflection following a coaching session.

Family-Centered Framework for Engaging Diverse Families

Family-centered early intervention is a recommended service delivery model and help-giving philosophy for working with children with disabilities and their families (Bruder, 2000; Dempsey & Keen, 2008). Family-centered services assume family members are active partners rather than service recipients in early intervention and, as a result, should be respected in goal-setting and decision-making processes (Bailey, Raspa, & Fox, 2012; Bruder, 2000). Thus, family-professional partnerships serve as a key component in family-centered early intervention. Such partnerships can occur "through interactions that are sensitive and responsive to cultural, linguistic, and socioeconomic diversity" (DEC, 2014, p. 10). Further, practitioners can achieve the goal of building family capacity by engaging the family "in opportunities that support and strengthen parenting knowledge and skills and parenting competence and confidence in ways that are flexible, individualized, and tailored to the family's preferences" (DEC, 2014, p. 10).

These practice guidelines are discussed below relative to early interventionists' practice dilemmas. Please note Tables 1 and 2, which provide practice checklists for these guidelines.

Engaging in Sensitive, Respectful, and Responsive Interactions

Understanding and being respectful of diverse family values and circumstances lay the foundation for family-centered practices. One of the first steps for practitioners in demonstrating respect for diverse families is self-awareness of their views and biases. Negative perceptions toward families may result in misunderstanding and distrust in early intervention delivery (Harry, 2008). Thus, practitioners should withhold assumptions and judgments when they encounter families from diverse backgrounds and circumstances. The sample dilemma in the previous section regarding families experiencing economic hardship demonstrates the importance of focusing on where the family "is" in their current life circumstances and priorities rather than on what the practitioner might believe the family priorities should be. Instead, practitioners need to take time to listen, understand, and respect individual families' life circumstances, values, and beliefs. Though they may experience cultural shock when learning about cultures and life circumstances other than their own,

practitioners constantly should be mindful of appreciating multiple family diversity characteristics.

One strategy for gaining a better understanding and appreciation of family life is getting to know the family and using cultural guides or mediators in helping to understand families' unique life circumstances (Lynch & Hanson, 2011). One practitioner described talking through the importance of respecting diverse family structures with a coworker:

> So I had a staff member who had never conducted a home visit with a same-sex couple. She first refused to conduct the home visit as it was not something she was comfortable with. After my conversation with her, I had a better understanding of the practitioner's views about her fears and concerns of going into a home without a female figure. We talked about it from the aspect of family and how family structures are different. And how this is different from any of the other experiences that she had.

In this case, it was essential for the practitioner to acknowledge her bias and fear toward families with same-sex couples and to gain a better understanding through professional support. This was accomplished by the practitioner engaging in open and honest communication with her coworker while acknowledging and confronting her coworker's biases regarding family structure. Understanding and respecting family diversity is a critical first step toward family centeredness.

Secondly, establishing responsive partnerships with families is equally important.

Establishing responsive partnerships. Families are important stakeholders and active partners in early intervention; however, families with diverse backgrounds may experience difficulties in communication and collaboration with practitioners. Responsive collaboration and relationship building with families requires service providers to prioritize families' needs and goals (Harry, 2008) as well as their available supports and resources (DEC, 2014; Trivette, Dunst, & Hamby, 2010).

Respect, responsiveness, and reciprocity have been recommended as essential components of family-centered practices for collaborating with families from diverse backgrounds. They are effective practice components in establishing rapport and building positive family-professional partnerships (Barrera & Corso, 2002).

Relationship building requires the early intervention practitioner to demonstrate responsiveness to families regarding their unique circumstances through open communication. One preschool teacher emphasized the importance of sensitive and responsive relationship building:

> We had a meeting with the Department of Social Services (DSS) because this family had been sending all of this sweet junk food . . . and we kept sending home notes about our healthy snack policy. And we never sat . . . down to talk to them about why we couldn't be doing this. And the mother at the meeting explained: "You don't understand, we don't know if we are going to be here next week so we want her to have all this wonderful food and stuff." It made us realize that "we forgot to ask the questions!" So, we found out at the last minute that the family were undocumented and concerned about being deported.

This practitioner freely admitted that little time was devoted to communicating with and understanding the family in a respectful and responsive manner. Thus, the value of open, frequent, and honest communication with family members is essential.

Home visits can assist in the relationship-building process as well as asking families about their goals and expectations for their children. As one home visitor described,

> I went out and conducted home visits and asked families: "What are your dreams for your child? And what are the miraculous things that you see in your children?" It was really so cool to be able to get to know these families, see these children in their homes.

This practitioner recognized the importance of conducting home visits to gain families' perspectives before formal school events such as open houses or IEP or IFSP meetings as an important first step in relationship building. In other words, meeting families on their "turfs" can go a long way in developing a respectful and trusting relationship. In addition, partnering with cultural guides, qualified

> Respect, responsiveness, and reciprocity have been recommended as essential components of family-centered practices for collaborating with families from diverse backgrounds.

interpreters, and/or parent mentors can be helpful. It's critical to continually engage families in reciprocal conversations about their concerns and explain information about their child, their rights, and service system options (Barrera & Corso, 2002).

Moreover, when and where meetings are held are important considerations in the relationship-building process. Practitioners need to respect family availability and resources for attending. In some cases, it may be more convenient or less intimidating for families to meet at community locations such as public restaurants, family members' places of employment or homes, or other "neutral" locations other than the child's school or early intervention setting. Establishing relationships with families and honoring their priorities and concerns are essential steps toward achieving effective communication and responsive partnerships. Such partnerships should lead to opportunities to build family capacity for supporting their child.

Supporting and Strengthening Family Knowledge, Skills, and Competence

To strengthen parenting knowledge, skills, and competence, practitioners should focus on family capacity building. However, in doing so it is important to recognize the continuum of family engagement and acknowledge that all families have different abilities and resources for engagement (Rouse, 2012). Not all families have the resources to be as actively engaged in their young child's education and early intervention services, but all are engaged with their child. One practitioner aptly described this continuum of family engagement:

> I have empathy for the situations many families are in. For some families just getting to spend some time with their children is a big deal, because a lot of them don't even get that. Often some parents are working second or third shift, and their kids are asleep by the time they get home. And they don't even get to see their child, so how are they supposed to do an educational activity with their children?

This practitioner realized the importance of recognizing, respecting, and being responsive to individual family circumstances by understanding that engagement is different for individual families. Another practitioner noted that "you need to be sensitive to parents who are more concerned about getting food on the table or paying their bills rather than making sure they get to an IEP meeting." She/he also understood the importance of accepting the level of engagement at which any given family may fall.

Of note, some families are not comfortable in the school setting; they may be shy and uncomfortable asking about resources or simply unfamiliar with the school culture or the language spoken in the classroom. So, understanding and responding to individual family situations is essential for family engagement and for family capacity building to occur. Two elements that work together to ensure that families have equal voices in making decisions about their child are providing information and materials to inform families and offering ongoing coaching as needed and applicable to equip families with skills necessary to actively participate wherever they may fall on the engagement continuum.

Informed consumers. Practitioners have an important role in providing families with the knowledge and skills needed to facilitate their child's development and advocate for their child's needs and services. This ensures that families will have the necessary information to engage in collaborative problem solving with practitioners and make informed decisions for their child and family (Able-Boone, 1996; Thompson et al., 1997).

In particular, practitioners can inform families about their child's development and disability, evidence-based practices, and available resources and supports so family members can understand available service options. This knowledge and confidence helps families build their parenting and advocacy skills (Thompson et al., 1997). Moreover, ensuring that families are informed consumers leads to parent and family empowerment, which has been identified by Rouse (2012) as the most important aspect of family-centered practices. It is also one practitioners struggle with the most.

One practitioner described how difficulties with understanding written materials can interfere with some families' ability to become informed consumers: "Some families can't just go to their handbook and read it on their own. They need someone there to explain content because of their literacy levels." This practitioner demonstrated that being aware of and understanding family resources and needs is essential for building capacity. Effective interpreters working with practitioners in supporting families with limited English proficiency also can ensure family engagement and informed consent (Cheatham, 2011).

Individualized coaching. Because families can fall anywhere on the engagement continuum, practitioners may consider different levels and types of coaching strategies for empowering families. Specifically, practitioners may coach families during IEP meetings and intervention implementation and on parenting techniques and/or whatever an individual family may need or prioritize. Practitioners may work in an enabling/capacity-building model (as opposed to a practitioner expert model) to help families articulate their child's and family's strengths and needs and collaborate to determine the most effective early intervention plan for their family (Brookman-Frazee & Koegei, 2004).

In a family coaching framework proposed by Branson (2015), there are three critical components to successful family coaching: (a) the targeted goals are a priority for the family, (b) the coaching occurs in a relevant context, and (c) the practitioner includes time for feedback and parent or family self-reflection.

> " Practitioners have an important role in providing families with the knowledge and skills needed to facilitate their child's development and advocate for their child's needs and services.

When deciding which goal(s) to target with an individual child, it must begin with a discussion about family priorities (Branson, 2015; Byington & Whitby, 2011). For example, if a speech and language pathologist wishes to work on baby signs with a 16-month-old boy but the family wants their child to sit in his high chair near the table for family meals, the intervention goals should begin with helping the child sit in his high chair because that is what the family prefers. Not only does this action give families ownership of goal development leading to empowerment, families will be more likely to work toward a goal they have been involved in choosing.

The second component involved in family coaching is that the coaching occur in a relevant context (Branson, 2015). Practitioners can devote their time to observing and working with children and families within their daily routines at home or other settings as well as supporting families through the IEP or IFSP meeting process. In the example above, a practitioner may schedule a visit during family mealtime and coach the family in strategies to help their child remain in his high chair.

Finally, family coaching must allow time for feedback from the practitioner and for family or parent self-reflection (Branson, 2015). This may be done through a variety of means and applies across the coaching continuum. After coaching families either in direct work with their child or through the IFSP or IEP process, practitioners may encourage parents to identify what went well and what could have gone better. Practitioners and families may collaborate and problem solve together to create family confidence in their ability to accomplish whatever they and the practitioner are trying to do. One practitioner illustrated the need to be flexible in family coaching:

> We showed up at this home and they were like "you do not know my family or where I'm coming from." It made us uncomfortable, and we really had to work. It was very powerful. We are there to learn and ask questions. And to build a relationship.

In sum, Branson's (2015) coaching model may be applied across the engagement continuum and contributes to effective family capacity building.

Conclusion

Taken together, sensitive and responsive interactions, as well as supporting and strengthening family competence, are essential components of family-centered recommended practices. The dilemmas highlighted demonstrate that family-centered practices encompass both dispositions (e.g., sensitivity, respect, and responsiveness) and skills (e.g., collaborative communication, relationship building, and coaching). It is important to note that all 10 of the Family recommended practices are integrated to establish and maintain true family-centered practices.

References

Able-Boone, H. (1996). Ethics and early intervention: Toward more relationship-focused interventions. *Infants & Young Children, 9*(2), 13–21.

Bailey, D. B., Raspa, M., & Fox, L. C. (2012). What is the future of family outcomes and family-centered services? *Topics in Early Childhood Special Education, 31,* 216–223. doi:10.1177/0271121411427077

Barrera, I., & Corso, R. M. (2002). Cultural competency as skilled dialogue. *Topics in Early Childhood Special Education, 22,* 103–113. doi:10.1177/027112140 20220020501

Branson, D. (2015). A case for family coaching in early intervention. *Young Exceptional Children, 18*(1), 44–47. doi:10.1177/1096250615569903

Brookman-Frazee, L., & Koegei, R. L. (2004). Using parent/clinician partnerships in parent education programs for children with autism. *Journal of Positive Behavior Interventions, 6,* 195–213. doi:10.1177/10983007040060040201

Bruder, M. B. (2000). Family-centered early intervention: Clarifying our values for the new millennium. *Topics in Early Childhood Special Education, 20,* 105–115. doi:10.1177/027112140002000206

Byington, T. A., & Whitby, P. J. S. (2011). Empowering families during the early intervention planning process. *Young Exceptional Children, 14*(4), 44–56. doi:10.1177/1096250611428878

Cheatham, G. A. (2011). Language interpretation, parent participation, and young children with disabilities. *Topics in Early Childhood Special Education, 31,* 78–88. doi:10.1177/0271121410377120

Dempsey, I., & Keen, D. (2008). A review of processes and outcomes in family-centered services for children with a disability. *Topics in Early Childhood Special Education, 28,* 42–52. doi:10.1177/0271121408316699

Division for Early Childhood. (2014). *DEC recommended practices in early intervention/early childhood special education 2014.* Retrieved from http://www.dec-sped.org/recommendedpractices

Dunst, C. J. (2002). Family-centered practices: Birth through high school. *The Journal of Special Education, 36,* 141–149. doi:10.1177/00224669020360030 401

Harry, B. (2008). Collaboration with culturally and linguistically diverse families: Ideal versus reality. *Exceptional Children, 74,* 372–388. doi:10.1177/001440290807400306

Hoffman-Kipp, P. (2003). Model activity systems: Dialogic teacher learning for social justice teaching. *Teacher Education Quarterly, 30*(2), 27–39.

Lynch, E. W., & Hanson, M. J. (Eds.). (2011). *Developing cross-cultural competence: A guide for working with children and their families* (4th ed.). Baltimore, MD: Paul H. Brookes.

Rouse, L. (2012). Family-centered practice: Empowerment, self-efficacy, and challenges for practitioners in early childhood education and care. *Contemporary Issues in Early Childhood, 13*, 17–26. doi:10.2304/ciec.2012.13.1.17

Thompson, L., Lobb, C., Elling, R., Herman, S., Jurkiewicz, T., & Hulleza, C. (1997). Pathways to family empowerment: Effects of family-centered delivery of early intervention services. *Exceptional Children, 64*, 99–113. doi:10.1177/001440299706400107

Trivette, C. M., Dunst, C. J., & Hamby, D. W. (2010). Influences of family-systems intervention practices on parent-child interactions and child development. *Topics in Early Childhood Special Education, 30*, 3–19. doi:10.1177/0271121410364250

U.S. Departments of Health and Human Services and Education. (2016, May 5). *Policy statement on family engagement: From the early years to the early grades.* Washington, DC: Authors.

6

Parenting Under Fire
Supporting Military Families Experiencing Challenging Circumstances

KIMBERLY A. HILE
University of Illinois at Urbana-Champaign

JENNA M. WEGLARZ-WARD
University of Nevada at Las Vegas

ROBYN DiPIETRO-WELLS
ROSA MILAGROS SANTOS
MICHAELENE M. OSTROSKY
University of Illinois at Urbana-Champaign

Eleven-month-old Addie learned to roll over at 7 months and is now beginning to sit up with minimal assistance. Rebecca, a first-time mom, wondered if something was wrong when Addie showed some delays at 4 months of age, but Rebecca was worried that others would see her as overanxious, so she put off discussing her concerns with the pediatrician.

Addie's father, Wayne, an active duty soldier, is preparing for his third deployment. On a previous deployment, his unit came under heavy fire resulting in fatalities to several soldiers. Since his return, Wayne has been plagued by nightmares, but with Addie's arrival, these appear to have subsided. Wayne is always ready to help when he is home, and he loves spending time with Addie and Rebecca. However, in two months he will go overseas again, and Rebecca has noticed that he has begun to withdraw from his family. She views this as his way to prepare for the painful separation to come.

Rebecca also has begun to withdraw from Wayne in anticipation of his absence, and she can be seen investing all of her time and attention on Addie. She finally mentioned her concerns about Addie's development to the pediatrician at their last well-baby visit. He recommended that she reach out to her local early intervention office to request an evaluation, which was completed two weeks after the referral. It was determined that Addie has delays in gross and fine motor development with recommendations for both physical and developmental therapies.

> For military families, the combination of military-related stressors and the challenges of parenting a young child with a disability can be overwhelming and can lead to feelings of increased isolation and uncertainty when navigating military and civilian systems of services.

While families involved in the military are not unlike most typical civilian families, they commonly demonstrate unique strengths that enable them to adapt and be resilient to the many challenges they might face. These families tend to be flexible and creative in solving problems and addressing life changes, and they often feel gracious and appreciative of others. Many military families are strongly connected as individual families as well as with other military families (Crosby, 2014).

These strengths help military families cope with the physical separation that occurs during deployment. Frequent relocations are not uncommon for military families and often lead to social isolation from their extended networks of family and friends. In fact, according to Kendler, Karkowski, and Prescott (1999), Army wives with deployed spouses experience higher rates of depression, anxiety, and sleep disorders. Moreover, families may experience emotional and physical strains because of a parent's physical injury or disability; in fact, many more military families deal with emotional stress caused by posttramatic stress disorder (PTSD; Mansfield et al., 2010). These and other challenges can impact a parent's ability to attend to a child's development and need for services (Holmes, Rauch, & Cozza, 2013; Russo & Fallow, 2001).

Notably, regardless of a military member's status (e.g., active, select reserve, veteran), military families often experience similar stressors. It is important to recognize that the spouses of military service members tend to be young (approximately 72% of active duty service members are under 30; U.S. Department of Defense, 2014) and have incomes that may not enable the family to access formal or informal systems of support. According to the U.S. Department of Defense (2014), approximately 85% of military personnel are male. Additionally, 72% of military personnel are 30 or younger. Forty-four percent of the 1,076,046 children of military personnel were under age 5 (U.S. Department of Defense, 2014).

According to Aronson, Kyler, Moeller, and Perkins (2016), an estimated 220,000 active duty or reserve military personnel are caring for a family member with disabilities. For military families such as Rebecca and Wayne, the combination of military-related stressors and the challenges of parenting a young child with a disability can be overwhelming and can lead to feelings of increased isolation and uncertainty when navigating military and civilian systems of services. These families may experience challenges related to building relationships with early intervention/early childhood special education (EI/ECSE) professionals who may not be responsive to their unique family needs. Finally, some military families struggle with accessing timely and appropriate intervention services in addition to maintaining a continuity of services when they relocate or reenter the civilian community (Freuler & Baranek, 2016; Hulsey, 2011).

The 2014 executive summary of the *Military Family Lifestyle Survey* highlights the "military-civilian divide" (Blue Star Families, 2014, p. 4). This divide leads some military-affiliated individuals to believe that the general public (i.e., civilians without close ties to the military) is not aware of the impact of military life on their families.

While most EI/ECSE professionals may feel competent in supporting civilian families in EI/ECSE systems, they may not be aware of the unique needs of military families. EI/ECSE professionals are expected to promote the active

Table 1
Strategies to Support Children and Families

During deployment	• Plan for changes in routines and help families practice these changes before deployment • Use visual supports, including personalized storybooks (i.e., social stories, comic strips) • Connect with support systems both in person and virtually (i.e., family, friends, military/community organizations) • Plan ways for deployed parents to remain involved in decision-making and intervention • Use technology (i.e., Skype, e-mail, audio/video recordings of deployed parent) to connect with one another
To promote parental well-being	• Gather information about family priorities and routines • Support children's understanding of parental well-being; use children's books, dolls, and role play to develop children's understanding of other's emotions • Provide information about military and civilian services for mental health, support groups, and physical well-being
During relocation	• Help families connect to the EI/ECSE system after a relocation • Provide information about the new service area (i.e., phone numbers, contact information for Part C and 619 coordinators, information for local programs) • Review IFSP/IEP with parent and provide written, detailed explanations as needed • Review parental rights • Obtain permission from families to share detailed information, including assessment, planning, and progress information

participation of families in decision-making related to their children's services, including referral, assessment, planning, and intervention. These professionals also are responsible for helping families achieve functional and meaningful goals as recommended by the Division for Early Childhood (2014). Given these expectations for working with families, it is critical to consider how EI/ECSE professionals can support the unique needs of military families while also recognizing the many factors specific to a family's circumstances.

In this article, three unique experiences of military families who have young children with disabilities—deployments, relocations, and subsequent parental well-being—are described along with recommendations for professionals on how to best support them. Table 1 summarizes the specific recommendations. As we follow Rebecca, Wayne, and Addie's journey, we share strategies that are framed within family-centered practices and that enhance the capacity of military families to support their children's development and learning as well as positive family-professional collaboration.

Unique Experiences of Military Families

Three unique experiences that military families encounter include coping with deployments, navigating relocations, and attending to parental well-being.

Deployment

Over the past 15 years, family separations because of deployment have become a common occurrence for many military families. Issues related to family separations have been exacerbated by the fact that military service members often experience less "home time" with their families before being redeployed (Paley, Lester, & Mogil, 2013). During deployment when one parent is separated physically from the family, considerations are made for every member of the family because deployments not only create stress for the parents, they also can impact children's development and behavior. Notably, children learn to acclimate to their deployed parent's physical absence and they learn to manage feelings of fear or anxiety regarding their parent's safety (McFarlane, 2009).

Osofsky and Chartrand (2013) contend that even very young children demonstrate negative responses to the absence of a primary caregiver. It may be difficult

for children with disabilities to express how they feel because of communication, social, or emotional delays. Professionals who support military families in the midst of a deployment should pay special attention to the attachment between the primary caregiver and the child. How well young children handle separation from their deployed parent depends on the ability of the remaining parent to balance his or her mental health needs while maintaining a consistent routine for the child. Because young children rely on their primary caregivers to make sense of stressful situations, it is imperative that military families experiencing separations because of deployment receive appropriate and individualized supports to strengthen the family unit as a whole (Osofsky & Chartrand, 2013).

Rebecca quickly recognized changes in Addie's demeanor that she attributed to the physical separation from her father. To help Addie maintain a connection to Wayne, Rebecca began showing Addie pictures of Wayne every night before bed and talking about fun activities they would do together upon his return.

Parental Well-Being

Researchers suggest that parents' psychological and emotional well-being can support or hinder a young child's ability to cope with stressors stemming from military family life (Osofsky & Chartrand, 2013). Thus, EI/ECSE professionals need to know the potential impact of stress on both the deployed parent and the parent who remains at home. Moreover, parents returning from active duty may experience a range of emotional and mental health issues, including PTSD, depression, substance abuse, or suicidal thoughts (Bryan & Clemans, 2013). Another consideration is the possibility of a physical injury or disability that may alter the parent's appearance, mobility, and level of independence. These changes can impact the quality of parent-child interactions. As a parent readjusts to being home as well as changes in his or her physical or emotional state, the child may experience difficulty identifying and adjusting to these changes, therefore requiring additional support from early childhood providers (Holmes et al., 2013).

The parent who has remained at home and assumed major responsibility for the day-to-day needs of the family also may experience additional stressors. Not only are they likely to be preoccupied with concerns regarding the safety of their deployed spouse, they also are responsible for meeting the needs of their children (Gewirtz, Erbes, Polusny, Forgatch, & DeGarmo, 2011). Some of these spouses may work outside of the home, adding to the number of responsibilities. Although many military personnel and their families value self-reliance and independence, and thus may be reluctant to ask for help (Taylor et al., 2005), it is important that EI/ECSE professionals monitor the "remaining" parent's mental and physical well-being.

During initial home visits, Sal, the physical therapist, noticed that Rebecca was engaged with Addie and asked questions to learn how she could support Addie's development. However, during subsequent sessions Sal noticed that Rebecca had become distant and disengaged. She frequently checked her phone and appeared startled whenever it alerted her to an e-mail, phone call, or text. Rebecca also began looking tired and worn down. While Rebecca had indicated that she understood the recommendations that Sal provided for her to follow through with between his visits, he was not sure that Rebecca regularly implemented them.

During one home visit, Rebecca burst into tears when she confided to Sal that Wayne's unit had been at a remote location and she had not heard from him for several weeks. She was worried about his safety and concerned about what he might be enduring on the deployment. She confessed that all she could do right now was to meet Addie's basic needs because her fear and anxiety over her husband's safety was all-consuming.

Relocation

During deployment when one parent is separated physically from the family, considerations are made for every member of the family because deployments not only create stress for the parents, they also can impact children's development and behavior.

Relocation presents challenges for accessing and continuing services for children with disabilities. According to Clever and Segal (2013), active duty military personnel relocate every two to three years, which is 2.4 times greater than typical civilian families. These frequent relocations mean that young children with disabilities who are eligible for services under the Individuals with Disabilities Education Act (IDEA) will likely transfer between EI/ECSE jurisdictions at least once by the time they enter kindergarten. As eligibility and availability of services vary from one location to another, military families must continually learn how to access appropriate supports for their family in a timely manner (National Council on Disability, 2011). Transfer and timely implementation of individualized family service plans (IFSP) and individualized educational programs (IEP) is vital to maintaining continuity of services. Additionally, the time and effort needed to ensure such continuity may be so great that many families may not receive the full continuum of services before their next relocation (National Council on Disability, 2011). Classen (2014) contends that to support military families during these transitions, it is imperative that special education professionals understand how to implement family-centered transition supports, which include being empathetic, using effective communication strategies, demonstrating professional competence, and engaging in collaborative relationships with families and other service providers. Using family-centered support during transitions from EI to ECSE systems (Branson & Bingham, 2009) enables families to better navigate state and local programs and experience continuity of services without becoming overwhelmed. It also helps children experience positive developmental outcomes.

Although there were no immediate plans for Wayne, Rebecca, and Addie to relocate, Sal began helping Rebecca consider how she might teach new service providers about not only Addie's needs but the needs of the entire family in case they had to move. Rebecca admitted that she was anxious about starting over with Addie's services in a new location, but she felt empowered to advocate for her family's needs.

Strategies for Supporting Families Within EI/ECSE Services

To support the engagement of military families in their children's learning and education, it is critical that EI/ECSE professionals recognize factors that may impact families and then provide the appropriate resources to these families. First, tools such as those available from the Early Childhood Technical Assistance Center (n.d.) are helpful for ensuring that professionals appropriately consider families' goals, priorities, and routines. A. Turnbull, R. Turnbull, Erwin, Soodak, and Shogren (2015) recommend that professionals approach their initial interactions with families using the following principles of partnership: communication, respect, equality, competence, advocacy, commitment, and trust. For military families, building respect and trust with professionals may be key to successful collaboration. The "military-civilian divide" described earlier (Blue Star Families, 2014) may cause some military families to distrust professionals charged with supporting their child and family as they often feel that civilian professionals do not truly understand their families' unique needs.

An additional consideration that may impact military families' ability to build respect and trust with professionals is the transient nature of the military lifestyle. In a report by Booth et al. (2007), adults who grew up in military families reported moving at least every three years, with 15% reporting that they had moved at least 11 times throughout their childhood. Families that are forced to change service providers numerous times may experience issues with trusting new professionals depending on the care they received in the past. Professionals also should be responsive to the ideals and values of military culture and realize that these ideals may differ from those of many civilian families (Taylor et al., 2005).

> "
>
> Because military families experience frequent transitions, it is vital for professionals to continually assess families' needs and provide appropriate resources.

In the vignette, it is clear that once Wayne is deployed, Rebecca's concerns about his well-being take priority over her ability to focus on Addie's therapy needs.

Second, enhancing children's social and emotional competence is key for military families so young children can develop the skills needed to cope with challenging situations. According to De Pedro et al. (2011), many military children experience adverse psychological effects because of deployments, parental PTSD, and changing family dynamics. While civilian children may also experience challenging situations, the stressors for military children may be recurring because of the nature of military life. For example, Hosek, Kavanagh, and Miller (2006) suggest that military families can expect to experience more frequent deployments because of ongoing military involvement in conflicts around the world. Providing children with rich emotional environments and nurturing their communication skills can support a child's ability to better express his or her feelings and ask for help when needed. Resources related to supporting social and emotional development can be found on the websites of the Center on the Social

and Emotional Foundations for Early Learning (http://csefel.vanderbilt.edu/) and the Technical Assistance Center on Social Emotional Intervention for Young Children (http://challengingbehavior.fmhi.usf.edu/). Using children's books related to social emotional development as well as books that focus on military life is a natural way to incorporate support into families' daily routines (see Tables 2).

Third, because military families experience frequent transitions, it is vital for professionals to continually assess families' needs and provide appropriate resources (see Table 3). Professionals should build relationships with others who provide community and military services in their area. This includes gathering information on military-based services such as:

- Exceptional Family Member Program (EFMP)
  http://www.militaryonesource.mil/efmp
- Tricare benefits and the Extended Care Health Option (ECHO)
  http://www.military.com/benefits/tricare/tricare-extended-care-health-option.html
- Army Community Service
  http://myarmybenefits.us.army.mil/Home/Benefit_Library/Federal_Benefits_Page/Army_Community_Service_(ACS).html?serv=149
- Fleet and Family Support Service
  http://cnic.navy.mil/ffr/family_readiness/fleet_and_family_support_program.html

Table 2
Recommended Children's Books About Military Life

H is for Honor: A Military Family Alphabet *Devin Scillian*	This book explores the branches of the military and speaks from the heart about the honor, privileges, and sacrifices of military families everywhere.
Hero Mom *Melinda Hardin*	The moms in the book are superheroes. They do all kinds of things to help create a safer world.
My Mother's Wings *Sally Huss*	The boy in this story misses his pilot mother when she is deployed for duty. But she knows how to heal his heart.
My Father's Shirt *Sally Huss*	The little boy in this story is sad when his father is deployed, but he has a father who knows what to do with the help of his favorite shirt.
Night Catch *Brenda Ehrmantraut*	A story that connects families while they are apart and offers comforting hope for their reunion.
Our Daddy Is Invincible! *Shannon Maxwell*	Based on the true story of a Wounded Warrior and American hero and his family.
Home Again *Dorinda Silver Williams*	Sharing this book can help a family readjust to life together after a long separation.
Why Is Dad So Mad?/Why Is Mom So Mad? *Seth Kastle*	This narrative story is told from the point of view of a family (parent and children) of a service member who struggles with PTSD and its symptoms.
Daddy's Home *Carolina Nadel*	A picture book that helps military parents explain the invisible wounds of war, including PTSD, to their small children.

- Family Advocacy Program
  http://www.militaryonesource.mil/
  phases-military-leadership?content_id=266712
- Child Youth Services
  https://www.armymwr.com/programs-and-services/family-assist/

Staff at these programs can recommend resources for parents as they adjust to new surroundings or experiences. Providing information about child care options, including those on military installations ("on-base") and Head Start, as well as subsidies and respite services, could be extremely valuable to families.

To maintain continuity, it is important to encourage families to retain relationships with extended family members and close friends they find to be

Table 3
Resources for Professionals Working With Military Families

U.S. Army Educational and Developmental Intervention Services (EDIS) https://www.edis.army.mil/	This program provides services and support to families of children with disabilities. It also provides early intervention services to those families living on military installations worldwide.
Military Families Learning Network (MFLN) https://militaryfamilies.extension.org/military-families/	The MFLN provides web-based learning communities and online professional development for those serving military families in a variety of arenas, including early intervention.
Sesame Street for Military Families http://www.sesamestreetformilitaryfamilies.org/	A website with a vast amount of resources on many topics relevant to military families.
The Virtual Lab School https://www.virtuallabschool.org/	Online learning modules that allow professionals to build their knowledge of research-based practices in child and youth care and development. There are a variety of military-related learning modules within this website.
Zero to Three Military Family Projects https://www.zerotothree.org/our-work/military-family-projects	Zero to Three offers a variety of resources that help professionals serving military families. They aim to help professionals and military families more effectively care for very young children.

See also
Military and Veteran Family Support
https://www.zerotothree.org/early-learning/military-and-veteran-families-support

positive supports. Connecting military families with one another either in person or through virtual support groups can provide families with opportunities to share experiences and seek advice from others in similar situations. Additionally, Taylor et al. (2005) suggest that families seek out support through other neighborhood groups, such as religious communities. EI/ECSE professionals should try to develop relationships with other professionals in the agencies into which military families are transitioning to help ensure a seamless system of services. With a family's permission, sharing detailed information (e.g., assessment, intervention, progress) with the family's new providers can facilitate continuity of care.

Finally, for professionals to provide family-centered support, they must be cognizant of the unique experiences of each military family. There are several entities that can help civilian professionals learn about military families. For example, the Military Child Education Coalition (MCEC) supports military-connected children and their families by providing professional development opportunities for special education professionals, administrators, and families (Hulsey, 2011). The MCEC assists participants in understanding the unique needs of transitioning military families and advocates for the presence of a family-centered system of support as soon as the family arrives at its new location. The Military Families Learning Network (MFLN) is another organization that provides online professional development for professionals who support military families. The MFLN (https://militaryfamilies.extension.org/military-families) has concentration areas for community capacity building, family development, early intervention, family transitions, military caregiving, network literacy, nutrition and wellness, and personal finance.

> **Military families are resilient in their ability to welcome and adapt to change as well as develop close ties within their family and with members of the military community at large.**

During his deployment, Sal, Rebecca, and Wayne engaged in a lengthy conversation over Skype to address the family's priorities for Addie. They discussed strategies that Rebecca could use to support Addie during play and routines such as bath and meal time. Wayne offered some ideas for how he could stay in touch and participate as much as possible with Addie's early intervention services. He video recorded himself reading Addie's favorite books for Rebecca to play each night after giving Addie a bath. When possible, Wayne agreed to join the early intervention visits via Skype. Sal placed a computer on the floor so Addie could crawl to and around her daddy. Sal also connected Rebecca with another family in the area who recently relocated from a military installation. The families quickly became friends and began to lean on each other for support.

In conclusion, military families are resilient in their ability to welcome and adapt to change as well as develop close ties within their family and with members of the military community at large. Military families are more likely to experience changes in their family structure because of deployments, relocations to new areas of the country and world, and physical and emotional stress. All of these variables can impact a parent's ability to focus on his or her child's special needs. However, EI/ECSE professionals can support military families' success by intentionally using family practices that respond to each family's unique priorities and needs, building on the capacity of all family members to support their children's development and learning, and developing strong relationships through meaningful family-professional collaborations. With these special considerations in mind, professionals can support families as they navigate the many celebrations and challenges that military life can bring.

Note

This material is based upon work supported by the National Institute of Food and Agriculture, U.S. Department of Agriculture, and the Office of Family Readiness Policy, U.S. Department of Defense, under Award Nos. 2014-48770-22587 and 2015-48770-24368. Additionally, the contents of this publication were developed through a grant from the U.S. Department of Education H325D110037. However, these contents do not necessarily represent the policy of the U.S. Department of Education and should not be assumed to be endorsed by the federal government or Project Officer Dawn Ellis.

References

Aronson, K. R., Kyler, S. J., Moeller, J. D., & Perkins, D. F. (2016). Understanding military families who have dependents with special health care and/or educational needs. *Disability and Health Journal, 9*, 423–430. doi:10.1016/j.dhjo.2016.03.002

Blue Star Families. (2014). *Military family lifestyle survey: Executive summary.* Falls Church, VA: Author.

Booth, B., Segal, M. W., Bell, D. B., Martin, J. A., Ender, M. G., Rohall, D. E., & Nelson, J. (2007). *What we know about Army families: 2007 update.* Fairfax, VA: Caliber.

Branson, D. M., & Bingham, A. (2009). Using interagency collaboration to support family-centered transition practices. *Young Children, 12*(3), 15–31. doi:10.1177/1096250609332306

Bryan, C. J., & Clemans, T. A. (2013). Repetitive traumatic brain injury, psychological symptoms and suicide risk in a clinical sample of deployed military personnel. *Journal of the American Medical Association Psychiatry, 70*, 686–691. doi:10.1001/jamapsychiatry.2013.1093

Classen, A. I. (2014). *Needs of military families: Family and educator perspectives* (Doctoral dissertation). Retrieved from ProQuest. (UMI No. 1683360590)

Clever, M., & Segal, D. R. (2013). The demographics of military children and families. *The Future of Children, 23*(2), 13–39.

Crosby, K. (2014, October). Military family strengths. Retrieved from http://www.militarypress.com/military-family-strengths/

De Pedro, K. M. T., Astor, R. A., Benbenishty, R., Estrada, J., Dejoie Smith, G. R., & Esqueda, M. C. (2011). The children of military service members: Challenges, supports, and future educational research. *Review of Educational Research, 81*, 566–618. doi:10.3102/0034654311423537

Division for Early Childhood. (2014). *DEC recommended practices in early intervention/early childhood special education 2014.* Retrieved from http://www.dec-sped.org/recommendedpractices

Early Childhood Technical Assistance Center. (n.d.). RP products by type: Performance checklists. Retrieved from http://ectacenter.org/decrp/type-checklists.asp#checklists-family

Freuler, A. C., & Baranek, G. T. (2016). Military spouses caring for a child with autism: Exploring risk and protective factors. *Journal of Family Medicine, 3*(1), 1049.

Gewirtz, A. H., Erbes, C. R., Polusny, M. A., Forgatch, M. S., & DeGarmo, D. S. (2011). Helping military families through the deployment process: Strategies to support parenting. *Professional Psychology: Research and Practice, 42,* 56–62. doi:10.1037/a0022345

Holmes, A. K., Rauch, P. K., & Cozza, S. J. (2013). When a parent is injured or killed in combat. *The Future of Children, 23*(2), 143–162.

Hosek, J., Kavanagh, J., & Miller, L. (2006). *How deployments affect service members.* Santa Monica, CA: RAND Corporation.

Hulsey, A. (2011). Military child education coalition: Building partnerships and support networks for military children with special needs. *Exceptional Parent.* Retrieved from www.eparent.com

Kendler, K. S., Karkowski, L. M., & Prescott, C. A. (1999). Causal relationship between stressful life events and the onset of major depression. *American Journal of Psychiatry, 156,* 837–841. doi:10.1176/ajp.156.6.837

Mansfield, A. J., Kaufman, J. S., Marshall, S. W., Gaynes, B. N., Morrissey, J. P., & Engel, C. C. (2010). Deployment and the use of mental health services among U.S. Army wives. *New England Journal of Medicine, 362,* 101–109. doi:10.1056/NEJMoa0900177

McFarlane, A. C. (2009). Military deployment: The impact on children and family adjustment and the need for care. *Current Opinion in Psychiatry, 22,* 369–373. doi:10.1097/YCO.0b013e32832c9064

National Council on Disability. (2011, November 28). *United States Marine Corps exceptional family members: How to improve access to health care, special education, and long-term supports and services for family members with disabilities.* Washington, DC: Author.

Osofsky, J. D., & Chartrand, M. M. (2013). Military children from birth to five years. *The Future of Children, 23*(2), 61–77.

Paley, B., Lester, P., & Mogil, C. (2013). Family systems and ecological perspectives on the impact of deployment on military families. *Clinical Child and Family Psychology Review, 16,* 245–265. doi:10.1007/s10567-013-0138-y

Russo, T. J., & Fallow, M. A. (2001). Helping military families who have a child with a disability cope with stress. *Early Childhood Education Journal, 29,* 3–8. doi:10.1023/A:1011348620920

Taylor, N. E., Wall, S. M., Liebow, H., Sabatino, C. A., Timberlake, E. M., & Farber, M. Z. (2005). Mother and solider: Raising a child with a disability in a low-income military family. *Exceptional Children, 72,* 83–99. doi:10.1177/001440290507200105

Turnbull, A., Turnbull, R., Erwin, E. J., Soodak, L. C., & Shogren, K. A. (2015). *Families, professionals, and exceptionality: Positive outcomes through partnerships and trust* (7th ed.). Boston, MA: Pearson.

U.S. Department of Defense. (2014). *2014 demographics: Profile of the military community.* Arlington, VA: Office of the Deputy Assistant Secretary of Defense.

7

Setting Partnership Expectations Through the DEC Family Recommended Practices

OSIRIS STEPHEN
as told to Bonnie Keilty

[Under the Family recommended practices], there's supposed to be a clear line of communication and understanding of what each person's role in the relationship is. How to set expectations, more or less, and also being aware of the fact that you are dealing with families. It cannot be personal. It definitely has to maintain professionalism. But even so, there has to be some personal attachment. . . . The parent is always looking to the professional as the person to take the lead . . . and it shouldn't be that way. . .

Looking at [the Family recommended practices], there's supposed to be an understanding at the beginning of the relationship itself, [and with that] it'll form into a relationship because there will be constant communication. Parents are going to look for information [and] guidance. And that's one of the things that I definitely picked up on [looking at the recommended practices]. And also the fact that the communication is clear. Because parents will assume one thing and yet the practitioner will assume that they understand. . . . Parents may not really understand, but they are just saying yes just to agree. So definitely the listening and the clear communication is very important [to meeting the Family recommended practices].

It's up to the practitioner [to make sure services are provided within the recommended practices] . . . because they do know more in a sense of what they want to see happen. It's just a matter of them walking the parent through each step of what's going to happen, what's to be expected, how to set goals [etc.]. It's not a matter of "I'm going to come in and do this, this and this," and the parent's like, "Okay." It's a matter of like "This is what we're going to do together." . . . That "we" must be part of the language.

So even having a parent walk through [a routine]. A practitioner can say, "Show me what dinner is like. Let me see how you guys prepare dinner. What is your child doing? What are you doing? What are you paying attention to as a parent?" and watching the steps. That gives the practitioner a vision of what really goes on and where the child may need the support. If a parent [is] . . . in a rush or they have other things to do or they're preoccupied, that child gets lost. And whatever work the practitioner has done or put in place is also lost.

I think one of the things that will be challenging [about the Family recommended practices] for a practitioner is to use research. A lot of parents really don't understand when you're bringing research to the table. "This is research based; we've seen this here." And the language, you would have to bring the language to a point where the parent is there with you . . . to basically break it down into laymen's terms. Because as we know, like children, everyone learns differently whether it's through listening, through active participation, or reading. So, [practitioners] have to be conscious of their audience, which is that parent, and also take into consideration what that parent's daily activities are and how they play into it. You may be talking to a parent, but that parent is thinking "Okay, I have to get dinner ready. I have to do laundry." So how much information are they getting? If you're using research-based information, you may lose them.

One of the things my wife and I would do is that sometimes my son likes to cook. So what we did was bought him a kitchen set, and while we're cooking, he's cooking. Sometimes I take him into the kitchen so he can see what I'm doing; he can participate. So he's learning how to use utensils. He's learning how to cut a piece of bread or a piece of chicken; he's learning how to hold utensils. Those are things that we integrate into his daily activities while we're doing it. So simple things.

[Using the Family recommended practices] would impact [families] greatly in that it would give them a template of what to work with. What the expectations are. What they need to change. What things they need to institute in their home in order to get the changes they're looking for or to see the improvements they want. . . . Because parents put out a template like "Hey, I need to see my child walk three steps. I need to see my child do these things." But how do I play a role? How does the practitioner play a role? How do we make this happen collectively as a family? With the recommended practices, it gives them a template to work with as well as how to participate in the conversation with the practitioner.

My question is, for the parents . . . everything is always time sensitive for [families]. . . . I believe if there was something like a cheat sheet [of the recommended practices]. . . . Something brief. Something they can take a look at. One sheet that they can utilize that highlights the most important things in a five-step plan. I think that would be great! Because that's really what [professionals are] trying to do. You're trying to get [parents] to buy into what you're trying to offer. If they don't, it doesn't matter what you guys do, it's going to get undone. If there's no understanding of what the expectations are or what their role is, it doesn't matter what you do. You can keep working with the family until you're blue, you won't get the results you're looking for or what they're looking for.

8

Bridging the Gap Between Home and School
Supporting Parents to Use Responsive Practices in Daily Routines

Rebecca G. Lieberman-Betz
University of Georgia

Zhen Chai
California State University, Northridge

FAMILY-CENTERED EARLY CHILDHOOD SPECIAL EDUCATION (ECSE) SERvices incorporate several key tenets, including recognition that the family (a) knows their child best, (b) makes the final decisions for the child, (c) is a constant in the child's life, and (d) can choose their level of participation in the child's program. Additional tenets hold that the family's priorities drive development of child outcomes and families are diverse in their cultural backgrounds and structure (Grisham-Brown & Pretti-Frontczak, 2011). Specific provider practices defined as family-centered by Wilson and Dunst (2005) include (a) treating families with respect and dignity; (b) providing services that are individualized, flexible, and responsive to families; (c) sharing information with families to support informed decision making; (d) respecting families' choices regarding their child's program; (e) engaging in collaborative relationships with families; and (f) promoting families' abilities to draw on resources and supports to strengthen their capacity to care for their children.

Though the Division for Early Childhood (DEC) Recommended Practices (2014) for families incorporate these key tenets and family-centered helpgiving practices in their guidelines for working with children birth through age 5 with developmental delays or disabilities, special education services often become less family-centered once children turn age 3 because young children typically receive services in a classroom apart from their families. This presents specific challenges to the implementation of family-centered services. Early childhood teachers serving young children with disabilities have a professional responsibility to incorporate family-centered practices in their programs, thereby promoting family involvement and increasing the capacity of caregivers to continue to support their child's development, effectively bridging the gap between school and home. Unfortunately, competing demands on classroom teachers' time (e.g., curriculum planning, team meetings, and paperwork) can make implementation of family-centered practices a challenging component of a classroom-based program. This article aims to support classroom teachers' use of family-centered practices to enhance the capacity of families to promote their child's development at home and in the community.

Ms. Claudia is an ECSE teacher with more than 10 years of teaching experience in an inclusive preschool classroom. Ms. Claudia understands the importance of family involvement, but she has struggled because of her competing responsibilities. This year, Ms. Claudia teaches a 3-year-old boy, Charlie, who was recently diagnosed with autism spectrum disorder (ASD). Charlie's mom, Amanda, approached Ms. Claudia about concerns that they were not doing enough at home to promote his development, especially given his new diagnosis. Amanda was hoping for some guidance on what they could be doing while Charlie was not in the classroom or receiving applied behavior analysis through the local university clinic. Ms. Claudia suggested setting up a home visit to talk about Charlie, his progress, and the family's concerns and priorities. Amanda was enthusiastic about the idea and gave Ms. Claudia the days and times that worked for her family.

When Ms. Claudia arrived for the home visit, she was greeted warmly by Amanda and her wife, Rose. The couple guided Ms. Claudia to their family room, where they were playing with Charlie. Ms. Claudia started the conversation by talking about Charlie's accomplishments in the classroom. Both Amanda and Rose smiled and visibly relaxed as Ms. Claudia discussed Charlie's strengths. Ms. Claudia then asked the couple about their observations of Charlie, as well as their concerns. Amanda talked about how Charlie loved games that involved a lot of movement or activity, such as tickling, swinging, and spinning. Although they found "tickle" was a great way to get social interaction, they had not been successful in turning other preferred activities into social and communication opportunities. Rose added that they also noticed that Charlie spent very little time playing with any one toy; he would flit from toy to toy and did not seem to play with things "the right way." Finally, the couple expressed concerns about his communication and hoped for a way to take what they were doing in the classroom with the speech therapist and apply it in the home. At the end of the conversation, Ms. Claudia repeated their priorities as finding ways to (1) socially engage Charlie, (2) help Charlie play with more toys, and (3) help Charlie communicate his wants and needs. "Yes!" Amanda exclaimed, "That's it!"

Taking the time to learn about the family's concerns, priorities, resources, and routines will allow the ECSE teacher to better understand how to support the child within the context of the family *and* classroom.

Although Part B Section 619 services are typically provided in the classroom, the importance of the involvement of the family in their child's program is not diminished. ECSE teachers have opportunities to continue to involve families in multiple ways, including as informants and active participants in their child's program, not just as recipients of classroom information (Grisham-Brown, Hemmeter, & Pretti-Frontczak, 2005). Taking the time to learn about the family's concerns, priorities, resources, and routines will allow the ECSE teacher to better understand how to support the child within the context of the family *and* classroom. Learning how the family is already supporting their child will allow the teacher to build on that foundation to generate additional strategies, such as use of responsive intervention practices.

Responsive Intervention Practices

Responsive intervention practices are naturalistic strategies promoting sensitive and contingent caregiver responses to children's behavior, ultimately supporting children's communication, social-emotional, cognitive, and language development (Kong & Carta, 2013). Responsive intervention practices include a variety of strategies such as following the child's lead, establishing joint attention, imitating the child's behavior, balancing turns, and inferring and responding contingently to a child's communicative behavior; such strategies have been included in many early intervention programs implemented with young children with a variety of developmental delays and disabilities (Karaaslan & Mahoney, 2013; Roberts, Kaiser, Wolfe, Bryant, & Spidalieri, 2014; Yoder & Warren, 2002).

A recent research synthesis across studies of interventions using responsive intervention practices demonstrated positive adult and child outcomes. Ninety-five percent of studies reporting adult outcomes demonstrated increases in parent responsiveness, while 85% examining social-communication skills reported positive impacts on at least some social-communication outcomes. Additionally, 100% of studies examining social-emotional or cognitive skills reported positive impacts on those child outcomes (Kong & Carta, 2013). Supporting parents in their use of responsive intervention practices may therefore be one way preschool special education teachers can promote positive outcomes for their students and increase the family-centeredness of their practice.

Early Childhood Special Educator's Role in Promoting Parental Responsivity

Training parents in the implementation of specific intervention practices has been found to positively impact child outcomes and parent behaviors supportive of child development (Delaney & Kaiser, 2001; Kashinath, Woods, & Goldstein, 2006; Roberts & Kaiser, 2011) and may support generalization and maintenance of acquired skills as well as increase parent well-being (Ingersoll & Wainer, 2013). A large body of research supports the notion that parents can implement intervention strategies when provided support and that children

Table 1
Recommended Interview Strategies When
Conducting the Routines-Based Interview

- Put the parent at ease by being at ease yourself
- Maintain appropriate levels of eye contact when the parent is talking
- Avoid the use of jargon and ask questions if you do not understand something the parent has said
- Use active listening such as nodding and vocalizations to affirm the parents' words
- Let the parent know the positive things they are doing for their child and family
- Ask the parent how he or she feels about things
- Place paperwork in view of the parents so they can see what you are writing
- Make a personal connection with the family by sharing a small amount of personal information that is relevant and appropriate to the context
- Offer to stop the interview or change the topic if the parent becomes upset
- Remain nonjudgmental of family members
- Ask parents to describe specific routines if it appears the interview will take more than 90 minutes
- Show parents the desired level of detail of their responses by asking detailed questions at the beginning of the interview
- Address the following for each routine: activity of the child, activity of other children and adults, engagement of the child, independence of the child, social interactions of the child, and satisfaction with the routine

Adapted from *Routines-based early intervention*, by R. A. McWilliam, 2010, Baltimore, MD: Paul H. Brookes.

do benefit from parent implementation. Additionally, a study by Ingersoll and Wainer (2013) found ECSE teachers successfully conducted an established parent training that taught parents of children with ASD how to use naturalistic and responsive strategies to promote their child's social-communication skills. This study suggests that helping parents use responsive strategies is an important way classroom teachers can help young children with disabilities reach their fullest potential. Often, parents are taught to use responsive practices within their daily routines and activities (Brown & Woods, 2015).

Supporting the Family Within Daily Activities and Routines

Supporting families within daily routines is important because routine activities such as mealtime, bath time, and dressing occur multiple times throughout the day, providing numerous opportunities for children to practice across contexts (i.e., people, materials, and settings). Additionally, skills learned in these routines are meaningful for children and families and provide a predictable context for embedding responsive intervention strategies (Woods, Kashinath, & Goldstein, 2004). Studies have demonstrated that caregivers can learn to embed intervention strategies within daily routines (Kashinath et al., 2006) and that caregiving routines offer similar opportunities for families to embed responsive intervention strategies as play routines (Woods & Kashinath, 2007). There are some basic steps that can help ECSE teachers collaborate with families to implement responsive practices.

Step 1: Identify the family's routines. Different families have different routines or different expectations for carrying out routines. For example, the teacher cannot assume that every family member will sit together during dinner because some parents may have different work schedules and, perhaps, breakfast is when the family gathers together and shares what happened the day before. By discussing with parents their daily routines, the teacher will have a better understanding of what is going on at home, with whom the child usually interacts, to what degree the child participates in an activity, and what the family's enjoyable and difficult moments are (Salazar, 2012). Though there are a variety of strategies for teachers to use to identify family routines, one commonly used tool is the routines-based interview (RBI; McWilliam, 2010; see Table 1).

Coming back from the home visit, Ms. Claudia shared her experience with Charlie's speech therapist, Ms. Lisa, and together they thought about next steps for supporting Charlie and his family. Based on the family's priorities, they both agreed it would be a good idea to introduce evidence-based strategies to the parents to increase their responsiveness to Charlie during daily routines. They decided the first step was to learn about the family's routines, what was going well, and where they needed additional support. Ms. Lisa conducted the RBI with Rose at school after pickup.

Step 2: Select preferred routines to implement intervention. With the information gathered during the RBI, the teacher works together with the family to identify routines that provide opportunities to help the child practice targeted skills. It is important for the family to decide in which routines they feel comfortable embedding intervention. For example, nighttime during weekdays may be the busiest time for a family because they do not get home until 6 p.m. and would like to put their child to bed at 8 p.m. As a result, this may not be an acceptable time for the family to implement intervention on weekdays. The routine activities selected to implement intervention should be individualized based on specific family characteristics; should reflect the family's unique priorities, interests, customs, and/or values (Keilty, 2008); and should avoid causing any unnecessary disruption of their daily life. In addition, it may be easier for the parents to understand if there is only one embedded goal during a selected routine at the beginning and then gradually add more goals and identify new routines (Salazar, 2012).

> It is important for the family to decide in which routines they feel comfortable embedding intervention.

Ms. Claudia and Ms. Lisa analyzed Charlie's RBI together. Amanda and Rose had already found a great game to engage Charlie (tickle monster), but they needed a little more support to get social engagement and turn-taking during other activities and expand his toy play. Rose indicated that both parents were musicians and would like Charlie to engage in some musical activities with them. Through the RBI, Rose identified times during the day when they could work on embedding toy play and communication strategies. Ms. Claudia and Ms. Lisa felt they could help them embed responsive practices during some musical activities to support Charlie's development. Ms. Claudia scheduled another home visit with Rose and Amanda to observe what strategies they have already been using and collaborate on ways to integrate some new strategies into a music routine.

Step 3: Provide intervention strategies to the family. Woods, Wilcox, Friedman, and Murch (2011) suggested a learning cycle for teachers to help parents implement embedded intervention (see Figure 1). Though the amount of support each family requires varies and there is some flexibility of the learning cycle, generally the cycle includes four phases. It begins with observation, problem solving, and reflection. Before introducing any new strategies, the teacher should gather information on what strategies the family has previously used and whether the strategies worked. It is important to individualize the strategies and build on the family's current knowledge. The next phase is direct teaching and demonstration within routines. When introducing a new strategy, it helps when the teacher discusses the rationale with the parents first (Keilty, 2008; Woods, Wilcox, et al., 2011). For example, before suggesting the parents rearrange their playroom, the teacher could explain that putting toys in sight but out of reach may increase the child's opportunities to make a request spontaneously. Parents are active participants during direct teaching and demonstration, and teachers should value parents' input and respect their choices (Woods, Wilcox, et al., 2011). The third phase of the cycle is parent practice and feedback. During this phase, the teacher observes parents practice the strategy within the routine activity and provides feedback on what is going well and what could be improved. Finally, the cycle returns to the initial phase of observation, problem solving, and reflection. During this final phase, the teacher helps parents reflect on their experience with the strategy and brainstorm possibilities for generalizing the strategy to other routine activities.

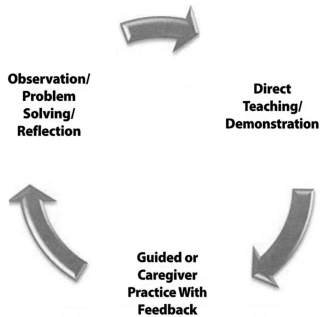

Figure 1
A Learning Cycle for Parent-Implemented Embedded Intervention

From "Collaborative Consultation in Natural Environments: Strategies to Enhance Family-Centered Supports and Services," by J. J. Woods, M. J. Wilcox, M. Friedman, & T. Murch, 2011, *Language, Speech, and Hearing in Schools, 42,* p. 385

At the next home visit, Ms. Claudia spent time observing Amanda and Rose play "tickle monster" with Charlie and their later attempts to engage him in play with some toy instruments. Ms. Claudia pointed out the responsive strategies they were already using with Charlie. During "tickle monster," Amanda would tickle Charlie as he laughed, then stop and look at him with a big smile. Once Charlie looked up at Amanda, she would start again, reading his cue that he wanted more. Ms. Claudia also remarked how they followed Charlie's lead during his toy play. Both Amanda and Rose's physical and verbal responsiveness indicated to Ms. Claudia that they were being responsive to Charlie's interests.

Ms. Claudia talked with Amanda about starting by first taking the responsive strategies she was already using and extending them to other routines or activities. Next, Ms. Claudia encouraged the couple to continue following Charlie's lead during play and suggested using additional responsive strategies, such as contingent imitation and narration, to increase Charlie's social engagement during toy play and ultimately expand his interactions with toys and caregivers.

Ms. Claudia modeled how she imitated Charlie's play with a drum while talking to Charlie: "Drum. Boom, boom, boom" as she hit the drum with the drumsticks. They both were playing with the drum as Ms. Claudia used words to describe Charlie's actions. All of a sudden, Ms. Claudia said "Stop!" and she stopped playing. Charlie looked at Ms. Claudia and stopped as well. Ms. Claudia smiled at Charlie and said, "Go!" Ms. Claudia started to hit the drum again and Charlie imitated her. Ms. Claudia encouraged Amanda and Rose to try the strategies and provided them with positive feedback.

In the end, Ms. Claudia asked if the couple felt like the ideas they came up with together addressed the family's needs; they indicated they could carry them out without too much additional burden on the family. Ms. Claudia told them she would like to know what was going well and to provide any additional support, so the couple should feel free to ask any questions during drop-off or pickup, or simply e-mail her.

Step 4: Keep ongoing communication. Successful implementation of responsive practices in home settings relies on frequent communication between the family and the teacher after home visits (Keilty, 2008). Parents need to feel comfortable asking questions, and the teacher needs to make sure that parents continue using the responsive practices introduced to them. In addition, as the child grows and makes progress, new goals may need to be developed, new routines may need to be identified, and new strategies may be added. However, it is almost impossible for ECSE teachers to conduct a large number of home visits because of their classroom responsibilities. As a result, parents and teachers may want to discuss other ways of communicating and conducting observations, such as e-mail, phone calls, Skype, text, or video.

> Before introducing any new strategies, the teacher should gather information on what strategies the family has previously used and whether the strategies worked.

During the next few weeks after the last home visit, Ms. Claudia frequently checked in with Amanda or Rose during drop-off and pickup to see how things were going at home. The couple were pleased with the new games they came up with to encourage social engagement with Charlie; they were even more excited when Charlie recently started vocalizing more frequently as part of his communication to continue the fun. Amanda noticed Charlie played longer with a toy when she imitated what he was doing and sometimes looked at her toy. They sent Ms. Claudia a video of how the three were playing with different musical instruments together, and Charlie was the one who was in charge of stopping and continuing the activity, with his parents following along. The couple also asked Ms. Claudia what they should do next to try to get him to do something more with the toys. Ms. Claudia gave some ideas for expanding his play with what seemed to be his most preferred objects and possibilities to use the same strategies in other routine activities.

Final Thoughts

ECSE teachers carry out a large number of diverse tasks, including managing the caseloads of their students with individualized education programs (IEPs), curriculum planning for students with and without disabilities that aligns with state education standards, individualizing instruction for students with IEPs, data collection, planning and participating in team meetings, collaborating with classroom staff and related service providers, and participating in the activities and culture of the school. Faced with myriad roles and responsibilities, it is understandable that challenges exist for implementing family-centered classroom-based programs. Nonetheless, supporting families remains an important part of ECSE programs, and this article is meant to help teachers identify ways that can promote family-centeredness in their practice.

Portfolios or assessment tools completed by the family (Bricker et al., 2002; Grisham-Brown & Haynes, 1999) can be a wonderful way to learn about all students' families and their perspectives on their child's education and plan activities that are meaningful for everyone. Providing families time in the beginning of the year to complete a portfolio or questionnaire can help set the tone for family involvement in the classroom from the outset. Ongoing opportunities for parents to participate in classroom activities (e.g., read/tell stories, cook a meal, do an art project, or lead music) are another way to increase family-centeredness of the classroom and elicit input from families to inform classroom curriculum. For some children, this level of involvement will be sufficient and meet their families' needs. However, some children and families such as Charlie, Amanda, and Rose will need more support and require additional activities and time on the part of the classroom teacher (e.g., RBI, home visits).

It is recognized that not every teacher will be able to make home visits because of time constraints or school policies. However, assessments such as the

RBI and current technologies such as Skype and video-recording cellphones allow for creative ways to conduct observations and gain an understanding of families' home experiences. For example, Skype would allow simulation of a face-to-face meeting to conduct the RBI, enabling participants to read one another's nonverbal cues, enhance communication, and build trust during the interview. Skype (or similar video conferencing technologies) could also be used to observe the parent implementing responsive intervention strategies and to provide immediate feedback. Preliminary research suggests distance coaching may be an effective means of supporting parent strategy use and enhancing outcomes for children with ASD (McDuffie et al., 2013; Vismara, McCormick, Young, Nadhan, & Monlux, 2013), although additional research in this area is needed. Alternatively, caregivers could video-record targeted parent-child interactions on their cell phone or tablet device, send the video to the classroom teacher, and receive feedback on practices via Skype, e-mail, or over the phone.

Helping parents capitalize on strengths and building responsive practices into families' routines through a specific set of coaching procedures (i.e., observe, problem solve, reflect; direct teaching and demonstration; parent practice and feedback) will support communication and social-emotional and cognitive development by extending learning opportunities beyond the classroom. When supporting families in this capacity, it is important that teachers do not overwhelm them with strategies (i.e., more is not necessarily better) and that the strategies for families are fairly simple to implement. It can be challenging to overcome barriers such as inadequate resources (e.g., time, staffing) and scheduling conflicts to bridge the gap between the home and classroom; however, implementing family-centered practices will help support development of the child and the family's capacity to promote their child's ongoing growth.

Ms. Claudia reflected on how increasing her family collaboration with Amanda and Rose had supported Charlie in and out of the classroom. She wanted to adopt a more family-centered approach for the other children in her classroom as well. To move in this direction, Ms. Claudia decided she would welcome back families after the holidays by having a family night featuring an opportunity to complete a family-centered portfolio. It was time to revisit her strategies for being more family-centered for all children in her classroom.

References

Bricker, D., Capt, B., Johnson, J., Pretti-Frontczak, K., Waddell, M., Straka, E., & Slentz, K. (2002). *Assessment, evaluation, and programming system for infants and children* (2nd ed., Vols. 1–4). Baltimore, MD: Paul H. Brookes.

Brown, J. A., & Woods, J. J. (2015). Effects of a triadic parent-implemented home-based communication intervention for toddlers. *Journal of Early Intervention, 37*, 44–68. doi:10.1177/1053815115589350

Delaney, E. M., & Kaiser, A. P. (2001). The effects of teaching parents blended communication and behavior support strategies. *Behavioral Disorders, 26*, 93–116.

Division for Early Childhood. (2014). *DEC recommended practices in early intervention/early childhood special education 2014*. Retrieved from http://www.dec-sped.org/receommendedpractices

Grisham-Brown, J., & Haynes, D. G. (1999). *Reach for the stars, planning for the future: A transition process for families of young children*. Louisville, KY: American Printing House for the Blind.

Grisham-Brown, J., Hemmeter, M. L., & Pretti-Frontczak, K. (2005). *Blended practices for teaching young children in inclusive settings*. Baltimore, MD: Paul H. Brookes.

Grisham-Brown, J., & Pretti-Frontczak, K. (2011). *Assessing young children in inclusive settings: The blended practices approach*. Baltimore, MD: Paul H. Brookes.

Ingersoll, B. R., & Wainer, A. L. (2013). Pilot study of a school-based parent training program for preschoolers with ASD. *Autism, 17*, 434–448. doi:10.1177/1362361311427155

Karaaslan, O., & Mahoney, G. (2013). Effectiveness of responsive teaching with children with Down syndrome. *Intellectual and Developmental Disabilities, 51*, 458–469. doi:10.1352/1934-9556-51.6.458

Kashinath, S., Woods, J., & Goldstein, H. (2006). Enhancing generalized teaching strategy use in daily routines by parents of children with autism. *Journal of Speech, Language, and Hearing Research, 49*, 466–485. doi:10.1044/1092-4388(2006/036)

Keilty, B. (2008). Early intervention home-visiting principles in practice: A reflective approach. *Young Exceptional Children, 11*(2), 29–40. doi:10.1177/1096250607311933

Kong, N. Y., & Carta, J. J. (2013). Responsive interaction interventions for children with or at risk for developmental delays: A research synthesis. *Topics in Early Childhood Special Education, 33*, 4–17. doi:10.1177/0271121411426486

McDuffie, A., Machalicek, W., Oakes, A., Haebig, E., Ellis Weismer, S., & Abbeduto, L. (2013). Distance video-teleconferencing in early intervention: Pilot study of a naturalistic parent-implemented language intervention. *Topics in Early Childhood Special Education, 33*, 172–185. doi:10.1177/0271121413476348

McWilliam, R. A. (2010). *Routines-based early intervention: Supporting young children and their families*. Baltimore, MD: Paul H. Brookes.

Roberts, M. Y., & Kaiser, A. P. (2011). The effectiveness of parent-implemented language interventions: A meta-analysis. *American Journal of Speech-Language Pathology, 20*, 180–199. doi:10.1044/1058-0360(2011/10-0055)

Roberts, M. Y., Kaiser, A. P., Wolfe, C. E., Bryant, J. D., & Spidalieri, A. M. (2014). Effects of the teach-model-coach-review instructional approach on caregiver use of language support strategies and children's expressive language skills. *Journal of Speech, Language, and Hearing Research, 57*, 1851–1869. doi:10.1044/2014_JSLHR-L-13-0113

Salazar, M. J. (2012). Home-school collaboration for embedding individualized goals in daily routines. *Young Exceptional Children, 15*(3), 20–30. doi:10.1177/1096250612446870

Vismara, L. A., McCormick, C., Young, G. S., Nadhan, A., & Monlux, K. (2013). Preliminary findings of a telehealth approach to parent training in autism. *Journal of Autism and Developmental Disorders, 43*, 2953–2969. doi:10.1007/s10803-013-1841-8

Wilson, L. L., & Dunst, C. J. (2005). Checklist for assessing adherence to family-centered practices. *CASEtools, 1*(1), 1–6.

Woods, J. J., & Kashinath, S. (2007). Expanding opportunities for social communication into daily routines. *Early Childhood Services, 1*, 137–154.

Woods, J., Kashinath, S., & Goldstein, H. (2004). Effects of embedding caregiver-implemented teaching strategies in daily routines on children's communication outcomes. *Journal of Early Intervention, 26*, 175–193. doi:10.1177/105381510402600302

Woods, J. J., Wilcox, M. J., Friedman, M., & Murch, T. (2011). Collaborative consultation in natural environments: Strategies to enhance family-centered supports and services. *Language, Speech, and Hearing Services in Schools, 42*, 379–392. doi:10.1044/0161-1461(2011/10-0016)

Yoder, P. J., & Warren, S. F. (2002). Effects of prelinguistic milieu teaching and parent responsivity education on dyads involving children with intellectual disabilities. *Journal of Speech, Language, and Hearing Research, 45*, 1158–1174. doi:10.1044/1092-4388(2002/094)

9

Adoption, Attachment, and the DEC Recommended Family Practices

DESERAI MILLER
University of Illinois at Urbana-Champaign

CATHERINE CORR
Vanderbilt University

KELLEY MUNGER
University of Oregon

CHRISTINE SPENCE
ROSA MILAGROS SANTOS
University of Illinois at Urbana-Champaign

Leah was born with spina bifida and spent her first two years of life bouncing between an orphanage and a hospital in a developing country. She underwent multiple surgeries, experienced painful immobilizations, and received care that was chronically unstable. When she was adopted and joined her family in the United States at age 2, she became eligible for services under Part C. Leah's parents were thankful for the support they received through early intervention. However, some of the services provided also conflicted with Leah's parents' hopes of building a strong and healthy relationship with their new daughter. During home visits, the physical therapist demonstrated practice exercises with Leah and instructed her parents to be the "therapists" during the week. Leah always did fine with the physical therapist during home visits, although Leah's mother wondered whether she internalized her fear and discomfort during those visits. However, when her parents did the exercises with her, Leah screamed, threw tantrums, and cried in fear.

Leah's parents recalled how this daily cycle created feelings of frustration, which were not helpful with their efforts to build attachment with Leah. Leah's parents felt confused about whether they should challenge Leah to be increasingly independent, as their physical therapist encouraged them to do, or if they should invite her to depend on them more because Leah had yet to form a strong, trusting relationship with her adoptive parents. Leah's gross motor needs were clearly a priority for her parents, but, as Leah's mother described retrospectively, "It would have been nice if the EI services we received had taken into consideration our family's situation. When physical therapy entered our world, forming an attachment practically halted. We're still recovering from that!" Leah's parents continue to wonder whether meeting Leah's emotional and attachment needs could have been integrated into the EI services they received.

For many adoptive parents, building a strong and healthy attachment with their child is the primary priority. Prior to adoption, many children who are adopted have not had their basic needs met regularly and have experienced inconsistent caretaking (Purvis, Cross, & Sunshine, 2007). When children are adopted, they need to learn to trust one set of parents and understand what it means to be a part of a family. Children learn to trust and attach by consistently and repeatedly having their needs met by their parents (Purvis et al., 2007). When a child is born biologically to a family and has minimal medical needs, the process of building healthy attachment can begin immediately through meeting the child's basic needs (Holmes, 2001). The child is fed by the parents, changed by the parents, and rocked to sleep by the parents; there is no expectation for independence at this point. However, at times, this process can look unnatural for adoptive families, especially if the child is not an infant when adopted. For example, adoptive families must meet their children's basic needs in the same way (i.e., rocking their child to sleep), but there is a balance between fostering independence and fostering attachment.

In this article, we describe the unique issues and concerns families face when they adopt young children with disabilities and how early childhood special education and early intervention providers can best support them to facilitate healthy attachment between parents and their children while at the same time meeting goals for building independence in young children.

Adoption of Children With Disabilities

Each year, thousands of children are adopted. Many adoptees are under 3 years old, and many have diagnosable disabilities or delays (Child Welfare Information Gateway, n.d.). Therefore, it is imperative that members of the early childhood special education and early intervention community understand how best to support children and families within the adoption community.

In 2015, of all international adoptions completed, families in the United States adopted more children from China than any other country (Intercountry Adoption, 2015). Of these adoptions, 90% of the children had an identifiable special need (Intercountry Adoption, 2015). Most children do not receive required care for their special need until the adoption is completed, which for many children means many missed opportunities for necessary surgeries, therapies, or supports. This makes early childhood special education and early intervention services even more important for families and children who have been adopted, but understanding the child's special need is just the beginning for many of these families.

Impact of Adoption, Disability, and Trauma on Attachment

The process of adoption presents many unique challenges to both the adopted child and the adoptive family. The process of forming a strong and healthy attachment takes time and effort. Additional factors such as a child's disability and trauma that may have occurred leading up to the child's adoption can further impact the already difficult process families and children go through as they

> Children who have been adopted are not only working on building healthy attachment with their parents, but they may also be managing symptoms related to trauma.

form those important bonds. In this section, we discuss attachment and how it is impacted by adoption, disability, and trauma.

For the purpose of this article, *attachment* is defined as a child's ability to feel safe and secure in their relationships with their primary caregivers (Purvis et al., 2007). For children to achieve a healthy attachment with their primary caregiver, they must feel certain that their basic needs will be met and that they will be kept safe (Kochanska, 2001). Healthy attachment in young children is the stepping-stone to attachment and building healthy relationships with others. Unhealthy attachment can lead to a child's inability to regulate emotions, build trusting relationships, and manage emotions, and it may limit feelings of safety and security (Levy & Orlans, 2014). Without healthy attachments, children have difficulty making gains in all aspects of their life (Kochanska, 2001).

Children who have been adopted are not only working on building healthy attachment with their parents, but they may also be managing symptoms related to trauma. All children who have been adopted have experienced at least one form of trauma, with many children having experienced multiple forms (American Academy of Pediatrics and Dave Thomas Foundation for Adoption, 2016). Some children may have experienced a traumatic separation by being taken away from familiar individuals and environments. Other children may have experienced many incidents of abuse or neglect (American Academy of Pediatrics and Dave Thomas Foundation for Adoption, 2016). Notably, children who grew up in unstable or neglectful situations often have difficulty feeling safe and secure (Purvis et al., 2007). Furthermore, young children who have experienced unreliable or aggressive caregiving stop trying to

get their basic needs met. Prior to their adoption, many children live in homes or facilities where they experience unstable, neglectful, unreliable, or aggressive caretaking (American Academy of Pediatrics and Dave Thomas Foundation for Adoption, 2016). Unfortunately, these circumstances can create an extra challenge for adoptive families on top of the additional needs children with disabilities bring to the family situation.

Adoptive families may find themselves working extra hard to build the trust of their new child, beginning with meeting all basic needs (Purvis et al., 2007). Secure attachment requires a safe and consistent situation, which is rarely what children who have been adopted previously experienced (Purvis et al., 2007). Additional interventions may be required to support the child related to the trauma, but the first step to healing is through healthy attachments (Levy & Orlans, 2014). Adoptive families, in theory, find themselves trying to make up for lost time (Kochanska, 2001); therefore, to build a healthy attachment, parents must

Table 1

Helpful Resources on Adoption for Families and Professionals

Books	
The Connected Child *Karyn B. Purvis, David B. Cross, and Wendy Lyons Sunshine* (2007)	A practitioner or parenting book focused on building trust and attachment. Considers the intersection between adoption and special needs.
Attaching in Adoption *Deborah Gray* (2012)	A parenting book focused on promoting healthy attachment.
The Whole Brain Child *Dan Siegel and Tina Bryson* (2011)	A practitioner or parenting book focused on brain development and regulation.
I Love You Rituals *Becky Bailey* (2000)	A practitioner or parenting book focused on incorporating attachment-rich rituals into routines-based activities.
Adopting the Hurt Child *Gregory Keck and Regina Kupecky* (2009)	A practitioner or parenting book focused on the intersection between adoption and special needs.
Children's books	
Baby Owl Lost Her Whoo *Cindy Lee* (2014)	Written for children who use control to feel safe. A proactive tool for teaching children how they can be safe even when they must share power with safe adults.
It's Tough to Be Gentle *Cindy Lee* (2015a)	Written for children who have difficulty regulating their emotions, understanding personal space, and understanding gentle touch. A proactive tool for teaching healthy boundaries and "gentle hands."
The Redoo *Cindy Lee* (2015b)	Written for children who need to practice healthy behaviors and habits. A proactive tool for teaching children the concept of "redo" when addressing undesirable behaviors.

make it very clear to the child that they are the individuals who will meet their needs (Purvis et al., 2007). This can be done by providing extra affection, meeting all basic needs, postponing a focus on independence, limiting direct and indirect contact with other adults, feeding and nurturing regularly, and respecting the child's boundaries (Cassidy, 2000; Purvis et al., 2007). Given these recommendations, the question then becomes, how can professionals in the early childhood special education and early intervention community support parent-child relationships while still providing services? How can early childhood special education and early intervention professionals serve as facilitators to

Table 1 (continued)
Helpful Resources on Adoption for Families and Professionals

Websites	
Karyn Purvis Institute of Child Development https://child.tcu.edu/about-us/tbri/	Information about Trust-Based Relational Intervention, an attachment-based, trauma-informed intervention for children who have experienced caregiver disruption.
Theraplay Institute http://www.theraplay.org/	Information about play-based, attachment-based intervention focused on growing trusting relationships.
Child Trauma Academy http://childtrauma.org/	Information about trauma-related training and intervention with children who have experienced caregiver disruptions. Focused on translating research to practice for children who have experienced trauma.

healthy attachment? In the remainder of the article, we address these questions by examining the Division for Early Childhood's Recommended Practices (2014) on working with families and discussing how these practices can be best implemented to support adoptive families and their young children with disabilities.

DEC Family Practices and Adoptive Families

According to DEC (2014), family practices are intended to (1) promote the active participation of families in decision-making related to their child (e.g., assessment, planning, intervention); (2) lead to the development of a service plan (e.g., a set of goals for the family and child and the services and supports to achieve those goals); and (3) support families in achieving the goals they hold for their child and the other family members. The DEC Recommended Practices emphasize the critical role of the family in supporting their child's development and the necessity for family and professional collaboration. This is particularly important when considering a child whose attachment and previous relationships have been disrupted. Therefore, the individual characteristics and expectations for each family must be recognized and respected (Trivette & Banerjee, 2015).

While many professionals have not had specific instruction or training in attachment-based intervention, a willingness to be open to hearing the family's strengths, needs, and priorities can create a strong and necessary foundation for the collaboration. Furthermore, healthy attachment between a child and caregiver can be built, supported, and encouraged by using the DEC Family recommended practices. However, in Leah's case and for many other families like hers, early childhood professionals must be intentional and thoughtful about how they deliver services. Below, we consider the Family recommended practices and how we can use these practices to better meet the needs of adoptive families.

Practitioners are responsive to the family's concerns. In Leah's case, the family's main priority was attachment. Healthy attachment leads to feelings of safety and security (Kochanska, 2001). For Leah, all previous relationships were severed, which created an increased need to focus on building attachment. If Leah does not build healthy attachments to her primary caregivers, her adoptive parents, she may have difficulty regulating emotions (Kochanska, 2001) or building trusting relationships with others in the future (Howes, Galinsky, & Kontos, 1998). Without healthy attachment, children may begin seeking out unhealthy ways of having their needs met (Howes et al., 1998), which can lead to very little time for skill acquisition.

When working with adoptive families, it is imperative we focus on attachment-based practices. For early childhood special education and early intervention professionals, this may mean serving in a coaching role and limiting direct contact with the child (McWilliam, 2010; Rush & Shelden, 2011). This allows for the relationship between the child and parents to strengthen while also providing necessary services. This approach limits potential confusion for

the child in terms of understanding who her primary caretakers are, and it allows for the family to make informed decisions based on their child's needs.

Practitioners support family confidence. Helping Leah's parents understand that Leah's behavior throughout the week was a form of communication and providing ideas for Leah's parents to be responsive to this communication instead of "pushing through" would have been a valuable opportunity for Leah to continue to develop a healthy sense of self and for her parents to increase their confidence in caring for Leah. It is imperative that early childhood special education and early intervention professionals empower parents to feel confident and secure in their role as the parent. In Leah's case, incorporating gross motor skill development activities while maintaining the primary focus on attachment was essential. Empowering Leah's parents to focus on attachment while being responsive to her gross motor needs may have allowed for more gains during physical therapy sessions.

Practitioners individualize services and encourage self-advocacy. For Leah, having goals that only addressed her gross motor delay was another missed opportunity. Incorporating Leah's attachment needs along with her gross motor needs may have enhanced both domains of development. Perhaps an interdisciplinary team could have developed a plan to encourage attachment while also improving her gross motor skills. For example, incorporating eye contact, warm voice, and playful games while implementing her therapy plan may have been beneficial to both Leah and her parents. Additionally, increasing the structure and predictability of each session could create a sense of safety, which is a necessary component in working toward healthy attachment.

Connecting Leah's parents to formal supports for families dealing with multiple challenges—in their case both trauma and spina bifida—may have been critical in helping them cope with the tremendous changes impacting their family. In Table 1, we provide resources for families and for early childhood special education and early intervention professionals to use while working with adoptive families. Finally, in the spirit of family-centered practices, meeting the needs of "the whole child" meant many things for Leah's family. For example, the spina bifida diagnosis, her attachment needs, her language and cultural needs, and any related trauma needs should all be addressed in an integrated way through a comprehensive plan.

Conclusion

The field of early childhood special education and early intervention has a rich history of honoring the importance of families in the lives of their children, supporting seamless transitions, and enhancing the parent-child relationship. For adoptive families of young children with disabilities, early childhood special education and early intervention professionals have a critical role and opportunity to help families build a strong and healthy attachment with their young children. With preparation and awareness regarding the specialized needs of adopted children, members of the early childhood special education and early intervention community have an obligation to provide integrated services that fit the families' needs and optimize early development.

References

American Academy of Pediatrics and Dave Thomas Foundation for Adoption. (2016). *Parenting after trauma: Understanding your child's needs: A guide for foster and adoptive parents*. Retrieved from https://www.aap.org/en-us/advocacy-and-policy/aap-health-initiatives/healthy-foster-care-america/documents/familyhandout.pdf

Bailey, B. A. (2000). *I love you rituals*. New York, NY: Harper Collins.

Cassidy, J. (2000). The complexity of the caregiving system: A perspective from attachment theory. *Psychological Inquiry, 11*, 86–91.

Child Welfare Information Gateway. (n.d.). Adoption statistics. Retrieved on November 16, 2016, from https://www.childwelfare.gov/topics/systemwide/statistics/adoption/#gen

Division for Early Childhood. (2014). *DEC recommended practices in early intervention/early childhood special education 2014*. Retrieved from http://www.dec-sped.org/recommendedpractices

Gray, D. (2012). *Attaching in adoption: Practical tools for today's parents*. Philadelphia, PA: Jessica Kingsley.

Holmes, J. (2001). *The search for the secure base: Attachment theory and psychotherapy*. New York, NY: Routledge.

Howes, C., Galinsky, E., & Kontos, S. (1998). Child care caregiver sensitivity and attachment. *Social Development, 7*, 25–36. doi:10.1111/1467-9507.00048

Intercountry Adoption. (2015). *FY 2015 annual report on intercountry adoption.* Retrieved on November 16, 2016, from https://travel.state.gov/content/adoptionsabroad/en/about-us/statistics.html

Keck, G. C., & Kupecky, R. M. (2009). *Adopting the hurt child: Hope for families with special-needs kids* (3rd ed.). Colorado Springs, CO: NavPress.

Kochanska, G. (2001). Emotional development in children with different attachment histories: The first three years. *Child Development, 72,* 474–490. doi:10.1111/1467-8624.00291

Lee, C. R. (2014). *Baby owl lost her whoo.* Seattle, WA: CreateSpace.

Lee, C. R. (2015a). *It's tough to be gentle: A dragon's tale.* Seattle, WA: CreateSpace.

Lee, C. R. (2015b). *The redoo roo.* Seattle, WA: CreateSpace.

Levy, T., & Orlans, M. (2014). *Attachment, treatment, and healing: Understanding and treating attachment disorder in children, families and adults* (2nd ed.). Philadelphia, PA: Jessica Kingsley.

McWilliam, R. A. (2010). *Routines-based early intervention: Supporting young children and their families.* Baltimore, MD: Paul H. Brookes.

Purvis, K. B., Cross, D. R., & Sunshine, W. L. (2007). *The connected child: Bring hope and healing to your adoptive family.* New York, NY: McGraw-Hill Books.

Rush, D. D., & Shelden, M. L. (2011). *The early childhood coaching handbook.* Baltimore, MD: Paul H. Brookes.

Siegel, D. J., & Bryson, T. P. (2011). *The whole-brain child: 12 revolutionary strategies to nurture your child's developing mind.* New York, NY: Random House.

Trivette, C. M., & Banerjee, R. (2015). Using the recommended practices to build parent competence and confidence. In *DEC recommended practices: Enhancing services for young children with disabilities and their families* (pp. 65–75). Los Angeles, CA: Division for Early Childhood.

10

Discourse During
IEP Decision-Making
Saying, Doing, and Being With Families From Diverse Backgrounds

CHRISTINE L. HANCOCK
University of Kansas

MARGARET R. BENEKE
University of Washington

GREGORY A. CHEATHAM
University of Kansas

At the start of the year, Barb and Alex enrolled their youngest child, Joe, in Ms. Ross's inclusive preschool classroom. Barb, Alex, and Joe speak a language other than English at home, but they are all competent English speakers. Joe is a caring and inquisitive boy who has an individualized education plan (IEP) for developmental delays in social emotional and communication domains. Joe exhibits challenging behaviors during center time. When Joe attempts to play with peers, he screams and stomps his feet. As Ms. Ross prepares for Joe's IEP meeting, she considers her relationship with Barb and Alex. They are polite, but they are hesitant to share. Ms. Ross wonders what she can do to engage them in meaningful decision-making. Meanwhile, Barb and Alex leave home for the meeting. "Ready?" asks Barb. "It doesn't matter," says Alex. "They never really ask what we want. All we do is sit and listen."

Family-professional partnerships are foundational to early childhood special education (ECSE) and recommended by the Division for Early Childhood (Division for Early Childhood [DEC], 2010, 2014). Partnerships can be demonstrated through shared decision-making where mutual trust and respect ensure both professionals' and families' expertise are acknowledged and built upon (Dunst, Trivette, & Snyder, 2000; A. A. Turnbull, H. R. Turnbull, Erwin, Soodak, & Shogren, 2015). Educators can learn about and act on family knowledge, priorities, and concerns as decisions are made (DEC, 2014).

As professionals, ECSE practitioners have the primary responsibility for developing family-professional partnerships. Without dispositions and skills, early educators may struggle to foster meaningful participation, particularly with families from culturally and linguistically diverse backgrounds.

Communication is at the heart of partnerships. Rather than language as a neutral conveyor of ideas, discourse involves saying, doing, and being (Gee, 2014) such that the words speakers use (what they say) have a purpose (what they do) and construct speaker identities (who they are being), which have consequences related to power between educators and families as well as equity of service provision. Words educators use play a key role in the extent to which interactions overcome immediate and historical inequities that marginalize families from diverse backgrounds (Beneke & Cheatham, 2016), such as the pursuit of shared decision-making.

In this article, we discuss how early educators' discourse in decision-making during IEP meetings can contribute to building partnerships or marginalizing families from culturally and linguistically diverse backgrounds. To this end, we first discuss issues related to power and inequity during IEP meetings. Second, we review research on discourse and decision-making during IEP meetings with a focus on Gee's (2014) notions of saying, doing, and being. Third, we explore how discourse can marginalize families when decisions are not shared. Finally, we recommend words that early educators can use and ways educators can reflect on their communication to enhance equitable decision-making with families from diverse backgrounds.

> Creating opportunities for equitable decision-making involves early educators' abilities to recognize and act on issues of equity and power between families and professionals.

Power and Inequity During IEP Meetings

Creating opportunities for equitable decision-making involves early educators' abilities to recognize and act on issues of equity and power between families and professionals. Power imbalances between families and ECSE professionals are inherent to interactions, often resulting in inequitable special education services for families and children from diverse backgrounds (Kalyanpur & Harry, 2012). Because communication is at the heart of interactions, a focus on educators' language use is critical to pursuing equity; likewise, language can be used to marginalize families when ECSE professionals place families in the role of being recipients of educators' decisions (A. A. Turnbull et al., 2015).

In the context of historical inequities in education and U.S. society for families who are considered "different" from the mainstream, families and children from diverse backgrounds appear most likely to have inequitable educational services (Kalyanpur & Harry, 2012). For example, during an IEP meeting an educator may propose goals without respect for families' routines, beliefs, and priorities. Consider Joe's behavior described above: Individuals from Western backgrounds emphasizing individuality may prioritize Joe's ability to initiate social actions, while individuals from group-oriented backgrounds emphasizing collectivism may prioritize Joe's ability to control his reactions to maintain group functioning (Chen, 2011). A family who does not adopt an intervention designed to increase social interactions may be seen as indifferent or uncaring, when they actually disagree but feel unable to say so (Kalyanpur & Harry, 2012). Early educators are challenged to recognize family priorities when they are different from early educators' cultural norms and practices (Kalyanpur & Harry, 2012). However, by focusing on discourse, early educators can learn about family culture.

Discourse: Saying, Doing, and Being

We draw on Gee's (2014) definition of saying, doing, and being to explain the social processes and consequences of discourse during decision-making. From Gee's perspective, anytime words are spoken in interaction (saying), the speaker is engaging in action (doing) and taking on socially significant identities (being). Importantly, language use is never a power-free exchange of words (Beneke & Cheatham, 2016). Instead, as speakers use language, they construct identities and relationships of power. As speakers engage in saying, doing, and being, they can gain, lose, give, or deny access to social goods (e.g., status, acceptance, services).

The words educators speak (saying) during interactions with families play a key role in shaping decisions and maintaining relationships with families (Bacon & Causton-Theoharis, 2013; Canary & Cantú, 2012; Harry, Allen, & McLaughlin, 1995; Schoorman, Zainuddin, & Sena, 2011). Speakers also perform actions through their talk (doing). During IEP meetings, educators often act in ways that uphold their power in decision-making, such as informing parents about their child and soliciting token agreement with educators' goals, strategies, or placement decisions (Canary & Cantú, 2012; Lo, 2008; Vaughn, Bos, Harrell, & Lasky, 1988). Relatedly, families tend to act by acquiescing even if they disagree (Canary & Cantú, 2012; Lo, 2008). Speakers take on roles through talk (being). When educators construct identities during IEP meetings, they tend to construct themselves as experts and families as recipients of

expertise, furthering inequitable relationships (Canary & Cantú, 2012; Schoorman et al., 2011). Thus, discourse in context (i.e., what speakers are saying, doing, and being) has consequences.

Pervasiveness of Unilateral Decision-Making

Although DEC (2014) recommends that ECSE professionals use family-centered practices to actively engage families in decisions and demonstrate responsiveness to families' priorities and concerns, negative consequences often result from IEP decision-making with families from diverse backgrounds (Kalyanpur & Harry, 2012). When families from diverse backgrounds are treated as inequitable participants in decision-making, educators marginalize them by devaluing their knowledge, priorities, and concerns (Canary & Cantú, 2012; Harry et al., 1995; Schoorman et al., 2011).

All too often, decision-making with families from diverse backgrounds aligns with what Collins, Drew, Watt, and Entwistle (2005) describe as unilateral

Table 1
Comparing Saying, Doing, and Being in Unilateral and Shared Decision-Making

		Unilateral	Shared
Saying	When are decisions discussed?	Decision takes place outside of conversation	Decision builds from what is shared during conversation
	How is the decision-making process signaled to families?	Decision presented as information, news, advice	Opportunity for decision made explicit
	What is said about available choices?	Range of choices not addressed	Range of choices discussed
Doing	Who acts as the primary decision-maker?	Professional(s) without family input	Family-professional team
	What is the major action of the family?	Agreeing to decision	Discussing thoughts that contribute to shared decision
	What is the major action of the educator?	Informing family of decision	Asking questions and providing wait time to learn family knowledge, priorities, concerns
Being	What is the main identity of the family?	Recipient of professional expertise	Knowledgeable partner
	What is the main identity of the educator?	Expert professional	Knowledgeable partner
	What are the consequences of these identity constructions?	Family knowledge, priorities, and concerns are marginalized	Family knowledge, priorities, and concerns are valued

Note: This table expands on Gee's (2014) conceptualization of saying, doing, and being and Collins et al.'s (2005) characterization of the features of decision-making.

decision-making (Canary & Cantú, 2012; Harry et al., 1995; Lo, 2008; Schoorman et al., 2011; Vaughn et al., 1988). Table 1 presents a comparison of saying, doing, and being during unilateral and shared decision-making. The table outlines differences in when and how decisions are discussed. Each approach also differs in the actions and identities of families and educators and the consequences that result.

According to Collins et al. (2005), professionals' assumption that they have the greatest expertise lays the foundation for unilateral decision-making; as a result, the decision is typically independent of conversation with families (saying). This is problematic because the knowledge, values, and priorities of families from diverse backgrounds are not accounted for in the decision. Instead, the professional focuses on soliciting agreement and reports the decision rather than presenting a range of options from which to make a selection (doing). During unilateral decision-making, professionals act as experts and families from diverse backgrounds are relegated to recipients of expertise (being).

However, decision-making can be more equitable. Collins et al. (2005) describe this as bilateral decision-making, analogous to shared decision-making (Dunst et al., 2000). During shared decision-making, family knowledge, priorities, and concerns are integral (saying; Collins et al., 2005). Professionals solicit feedback, and families from diverse backgrounds share thoughts that are incorporated into a shared decision (doing). Professionals highlight the decision being made by making the options explicit (doing), and families and professionals construct themselves as knowledgeable partners (being).

Joe's IEP meeting begins, and Ms. Ross asks Barb and Alex if they have questions or concerns about Joe's recent behavior. When they are silent but nod "no," Ms. Ross moves on. She suggests the following goal: With prompting and visual supports, Joe will use appropriate words (e.g., "My turn") to communicate and interact with peers for 80% of opportunities during a 15-minute center time, as measured by direct observation and a behavior checklist. Barb and Alex nod in agreement. As the meeting continues, the team discusses how to address this goal.

Unilateral Decision-Making: An Example

In this section, we present an example of unilateral decision-making that marginalizes Joe's family by minimizing opportunities to share their knowledge, priorities, and concerns. Saying, doing, and being are highlighted to illustrate how words spoken, actions taken, and identities constructed can impede partnerships. Because words spoken are integral to discourse, we present a conversation between Ms. Ross, Barb, and Alex. When educators inform families of decisions and solicit agreement rather than present options and opportunities for dialogue, educators engage in unilateral decision-making (Collins et al., 2005), marginalizing families from diverse backgrounds by ignoring family priorities and values.

Saying

Ms. Ross: [looking at paperwork] Okay, now that we've decided on Joe's IEP goal, we need to determine how we will address the goal here in preschool.
Barb: [glances at Alex] Okay . . .
Ms. Ross: Based on the data that we've been taking and how we normally address behavioral goals, we're gonna continue working with Joe by using prevention strategies, such as circle time and reading a social story about calming down. All the kids could use a reminder about that. [short pause]
Barb: Yes, I— [interrupted by Ms. Ross, who begins speaking at the same time]
Ms. Ross: Let's see, and we talked about this already. We're going to address his behavior by teaching Joe about a visual support that prompts him to use his words to join in with play. We have a few social stories already made; we'll make a few more. During center time, a teacher will be close to Joe to prompt him using the visual card as he enters a center. The teacher will watch for cues he's getting

upset. When we see this, we'll prompt him with the card. [short pause]
Barb: Okay . . .
Alex: That seems like it would work . . . [interrupted by Ms. Ross, who begins speaking at the same time]
Ms. Ross: Now, let's talk about paperwork.

Doing

Analysis of words spoken in the transcript (saying) provides insight into actions taken by Ms. Ross, Barb, and Alex (doing). Ms. Ross informs Barb and Alex about the strategies to address Joe's behavior. Ms. Ross presents her plans as already-decided, making it difficult for Barb and Alex to question her choices or add ideas.

She refers to earlier conversation to move forward without discussion. By speaking in long phrases with few pauses, Ms. Ross does not allow Joe's parents to initiate dialogue. Barb and Alex are placed in a position where they are expected to act by providing agreement, which they provide. Yet it is unclear how much they support this plan because Ms. Ross interrupts several times, silencing them to advance the conversation.

Being

By examining words spoken (saying) and actions taken (doing), we can now consider roles taken on by Ms. Ross, Barb, and Alex (being). Ms. Ross uses professional power to construct her identity as an expert. Given the narrow boundaries for negotiating how to address Joe's goal, Barb and Alex construct identities as recipients of expertise. Ms. Ross minimizes opportunities for Barb and Alex to contribute regarding the value of using visual supports with Joe. These limited opportunities to participate in decision-making decrease the potential for Barb and Alex to be recognized as competent parents with important insights.

Joe's parents could have shared their priorities for managing behavior and engaging in play as they relate to their cultural values (Chen, 2011). However, Ms. Ross's use of unilateral decision-making results in an inequitable relationship. Family knowledge, priorities, and concerns go unheard, and, as a result, the strategies for Joe's goal do not adequately represent him or his needs. Ultimately, this process further marginalizes Barb, Alex, and Joe as a family from a diverse cultural background.

Recommendations for Shared Decision-Making

In the following section, we present recommendations for educators to engage in shared decision-making. We present an example transcript illustrating shared decision-making during an IEP meeting and questions for educator reflection on shared decision-making.

A Shared Decision-Making Example

Educators' talk is integral to shared decision-making. In discussion of the transcript of talk between Ms. Ross and Joe's parents, we highlight saying, doing, and being to present strategies for words to use, actions to engage in, and roles to take on that support equitable family-professional partnerships. Several strategies to support shared decision-making are presented: making the opportunity for decision-making explicit, soliciting family feedback, providing wait time, and listening to and acting on family priorities.

Saying

Ms. Ross: What we'll do now is decide on specific strategies to help Joe [looks at Barb and Alex]. We have several options to consider, including any ideas you'd like to share [five-second pause]

Alex: Right.

Ms. Ross: So [short pause] here are a few examples of visual supports. This is a thermometer we could use to get Joe thinking about how he feels. [Ms. Ross passes behavior thermometer visual to Alex]

Barb: This would be nice to have around when he's starting to get upset . . .

Ms. Ross: This is a keyring he could carry around that has pictures of the steps for using his words to join in with play. And this is a sheet similar to the keyring [five-second pause]

Alex: [hesitates] Well [three-second pause] it's nice, but uhh [another pause]

Ms. Ross: [five-second pause] Please, go ahead . . .

Alex: It's just . . . for us, it's more important that Joe can . . . control himself.

Barb: We were just thinking maybe we would start by doing more to address the yelling.

Alex: We don't want him to be disrupting, or bothering anyone.

Ms. Ross: So, focus the strategies more on managing emotions rather than joining the play?

Alex: Yes. That's what we've really been trying to work on at home.

Barb: Like maybe the sheet could show him how to calm down instead?

Ms. Ross: Yes, yes, let's do that. That's important, thanks for sharing. Any other ideas? [five-second pause]

Table 2
Questions for Educators' Reflection Regarding Saying, Doing, and Being

Saying	• What do I intend to *say*? • How do I signal the decision-making process to the family? • How do I ask the family to share? • What information can I share to support the family's decision-making participation? • How do I share power in what is said?
Doing	• What am I trying to *do*? What are family members trying to *do*? • What is the purpose for the meeting? • How can I be explicit about what decision we will be making and what all of our options are? • How can I act in equitable ways toward the family?
Being	• Who am I trying to *be*? Who are family members trying to *be*? • How does my identity and cultural background shape what happens when I meet with families? • How do family members' identities and cultural backgrounds shape what happens when I meet with families? • How important is it to me that families accept my professional opinion? • How do I ensure balance in the power relationship between myself and this family?

Note: This table expands on Gee's (2014) conceptualization of saying, doing, and being.

Doing

Consideration of the words spoken in the transcript (saying) offers insight into the actions taken by Ms. Ross, Barb, and Alex (doing). Ms. Ross highlights the intended decisions, invites dialogue, provides wait time, and listens to and acts on family priorities. Ms. Ross emphasizes the decision has "several options" and invites Joe's parents to contribute and negotiate ("This is a thermometer we *could* use"). Ms. Ross asks for the parents' contributions throughout the conversation, and, as a result, they share their thoughts. Ms. Ross provides wait time and encourages Alex when he hesitates. When Alex and Barb share that they want to focus on managing Joe's emotions, Ms. Ross listens to their priorities. After Barb shares a specific idea, Ms. Ross demonstrates willingness to act on family priorities and incorporate the strategy.

Being

By examining words spoken (saying) and actions taken (doing) during shared decision-making, we now can consider some of the roles taken by teachers and parents (being). Ms. Ross uses her professional power to create conversational space for Barb and Alex to share (i.e., soliciting meaningful feedback, providing wait time). Ms. Ross constructs herself as a teammate and knowledgeable partner. As a result, Barb and Alex discuss their thoughts and also construct themselves as teammates and partners with their own goals for their child. Ms.

Ross shares power in the conversation, maximizing opportunities for Barb and Alex to contribute their parental expertise. Barb and Alex offer knowledge about what will work best for Joe given their culture, priorities, and routines. Given the multiple opportunities to contribute to decision-making, Barb and Alex are recognized as competent parents whose insights are valued. Thus, the features of shared decision-making help Ms. Ross equitably partner with Barb and Alex.

Reflection Strategies to Enhance Opportunities for Shared Decision-Making

By adopting strategies for reflection, educators can actively engage families in decision-making and demonstrate responsiveness to families' priorities and concerns (DEC, 2014). Table 2 presents questions educators can use to reflect on the words they use, the actions they take, and the identities they construct. For example, to reflect on saying, educators can ask, "How do I signal the decision-making process to the family?" Had Ms. Ross reflected on this in the unilateral example, she might have realized she obscured the opportunity for the family to make a choice. To reflect on doing, educators can ask, "What am I trying to *do*?" Ms. Ross wanted to engage Barb and Alex in decision-making. However, in the unilateral example, she acted by informing Barb and Alex of her plans, which limited how they could respond. Reflection may have helped Ms. Ross take different actions.

To reflect on being, educators can ask, "How do family members' identities and cultural backgrounds shape what happens when I meet with families?" If Ms. Ross reflected on this, she might have developed insight into communication with Barb and Alex, such as seeing their tendency to be quiet as related to previous experiences when their priorities were not valued. Through reflection, early educators will be more prepared to engage families in decision-making. Similarly, educators will be more attuned to the consequences of conversations and how discourse contributes to supporting partnerships or marginalizing families from diverse backgrounds.

> Through reflection, educators will be more attuned to the consequences of conversations and how discourse contributes to supporting partnerships or marginalizing families from diverse backgrounds.

Conclusion

Families from culturally and linguistically diverse backgrounds often face inequities in service provision within early childhood special education. Given the importance of family-professional partnerships, early educators' understanding of discourse during IEP meeting decision-making is essential. Through the words educators use, educators can shift power to families from diverse backgrounds. Through a focus on discourse and reflecting on their practice, early educators such as Ms. Ross can move to shared decision-making, which promotes partnerships that acknowledge family expertise and priorities.

References

Bacon, J. K., & Causton-Theoharis, J. (2013). "It should be teamwork": A critical investigation of school practices and parent advocacy in special education.

International Journal of Inclusive Education, 17, 682–699. doi:10.1080/13603 116.2012.708060

Beneke, M. R., & Cheatham, G. A. (2016). Inclusive, democratic family-professional partnerships: (Re)conceptualizing culture and language in teacher preparation. *Topics in Early Childhood Special Education, 35*, 234–244. doi:10.1177/0271121415581611

Canary, H. E., & Cantú, E. (2012). Making decisions about children's disabilities: Mediation and structuration in cross-system meetings. *Western Journal of Communication, 76*, 270–297. doi:10.1080/10570314.2011.651252

Chen, X. (2011). Culture and children's socioemotional functioning: A contextual-developmental perspective. In X. Chen & K. H. Rubin (Eds.), *Socioemotional development in cultural context* (pp. 29–52). New York, NY: Guilford Press.

Collins, S., Drew, P., Watt, I., & Entwistle, V. (2005). "Unilateral" and "bilateral" practitioner approaches in decision-making about treatment. *Social Science & Medicine, 61*, 2611–2627. doi:10.1016/j.socscimed.2005.04.047

Division for Early Childhood. (2010, September). *Responsiveness to ALL children, families, and professionals: Integrating cultural and linguistic diversity into policy and practice* (Position statement). Missoula, MT: Author.

Division for Early Childhood. (2014). *DEC recommended practices in early intervention/early childhood special education 2014.* Retrieved from http://www.dec-sped.org/recommendedpractices

Dunst, C. J., Trivette, C. M., & Snyder, D. M. (2000). Family-professional partnerships: A behavioral science perspective. In J. M. Fine & R. L. Simpson (Eds.), *Collaboration with parents and families of children and youth with exceptionalities* (2nd ed., pp. 27–48). Austin, TX: PRO-ED.

Gee, J. P. (2014). *An introduction to discourse analysis: Theory and method* (4th ed.). New York, NY: Routledge.

Harry, B., Allen, N., & McLaughlin, M. (1995). Communication versus compliance: African-American parents' involvement in special education. *Exceptional Children, 61*, 364–377.

Kalyanpur, M., & Harry, B. (2012). *Cultural reciprocity in special education: Building family-professional relationships.* Baltimore, MD: Paul H. Brookes.

Lo, L. (2008). Chinese families' level of participation and experiences in IEP meetings. *Preventing School Failure, 53*, 21–27. doi:10.3200/PSFL.53.1.21-27

Schoorman, D., Zainuddin, H., & Sena, S. R. (2011). The politics of a child study team: Advocating for immigrant families. *Multicultural Education, 18*(4), 31–38.

Turnbull, A. A., Turnbull, H. R., Erwin, E. J., Soodak, L. C., & Shogren, K. A. (2015). *Families, professionals, and exceptionality: Positive outcomes through partnerships and trust* (7th ed.). Upper Saddle River, NJ: Pearson.

Vaughn, S., Bos, C. S., Harrell, J. E., & Lasky, B. A. (1988). Parent participation in the initial placement/IEP conference ten years after mandated involvement. *Journal of Learning Disabilities, 21*, 82–89. doi:10.1177/002221948802100204

11

Mindful Parenting
for Everyday Routines
How Practitioners Can Help Parents
Reduce Stress and Be More Present

Tracy J. Raulston
University of Oregon

Sarah G. Hansen
Georgia State University

LISA IS A CERTIFIED EARLY INTERVENTION PRACTITIONER WHO PRImarily serves families, birth to 5 years, in home settings. She has training and experience working with parents to help them teach functional skills such as eating and toileting, develop play and social communication skills, and manage their child's challenging behavior. One thing she has noticed is that parents who manage frequently occurring or serious challenging behavior often have heightened stress. When she gives suggestions to families, Lisa notices they often report that "things are too difficult" or they "don't know if that strategy will work." In particular, parents may be overwhelmed by financial stressors, unable to find time to try interventions, or may be juggling multiple children and responsibilities. Although Lisa has a wealth of experience supporting families and is skilled at helping families strengthen parent-child interactions and relationships, there are some times when she feels that a parent's stress needs to be addressed before she can really make progress with the entire family ecology.

Mindful Parenting

One method that addresses parenting stress in a family-centered approach is mindful parenting. Mindful parenting involves applying a nonjudgmental moment-to-moment awareness during parent-child interactions and to the relationship as a whole (M. Kabat-Zinn & J. Kabat-Zinn, 1997). Specifically, mindful parenting allows parents to (a) notice and describe their physical sensations, thoughts, and emotions; (b) nonjudgmentally accept their child and themselves; (c) act with emotional awareness; and (d) respond instead of react to their child

(Duncan, Coatsworth, & Greenberg, 2009). Mindful parenting has been found to be associated with lower parenting stress, anxiety, and depression in parents of children with delays/disabilities (Beer, Ward, & Moar, 2013; Jones, Hastings, Totsika, Keane, & Rhule, 2014). Parents of children with developmental delays who have been educated in mindfulness have reported increases in life satisfaction, self-compassion, and well-being (Bazzano et al., 2010; Neece, 2014), and decreases in child hyperactivity, aggression, and noncompliance have been reported and observed (Neece, 2014; Singh et al., 2006). For parents of infants, a recent study showed mothers who participated in training on mindful parenting practices reported improvements in their well-being, parental confidence, and responsivity, as well as their infant's positive affect (Potharst, Aktar, Rexwinkel, Rigterink, & Bögels, 2017). These findings indicate that teaching mindful parenting strategies holds promise to increase the quality of life for the entire family unit. In the next section, we outline how mindful parenting practices can be taught within the context of early intervention and how practitioners, such as Lisa, can teach parents the beginning steps of mindful parenting as well as proactive and in-the-moment mindful parenting practices.

Mindful Parenting in Early Intervention

Early intervention practitioners meet with families of children with or at risk for developmental delays/disabilities to assess the needs of the family and child, develop goals, and guide the family through up-to-date, evidence-based interventions within the child's natural environment. Individualized Family Service Plans (IFSPs) involve the entire family unit. Early intervention practitioners are often faced with the question "How can I support this parent to achieve their goals for their child?" During the IFSP process, a parent might report to their early intervention service coordinator that their stress is getting in the way of implementing recommended strategies. In such instances, mindful parenting practices may help practitioners create supports for the parent to overcome this challenge while also aligning with the Division for Early Childhood's (2014) Family recommended practices on capacity building (e.g., F5, F6, F7). The practices we describe capitalize on parents' strengths, promote family confidence and competence, strengthen family-child relationships, and can be delivered in a flexible manner at no additional cost. These practices can also promote infant and toddler development by supporting parents to be emotionally responsive and facilitating a sensory and language rich environment (Reynolds, 2003). In the next section, we describe the skills early intervention practitioners can teach parents to be proactively mindful and some in-the-moment mindfulness strategies.

How to Begin Mindful Parenting

First, early intervention practitioners can begin by guiding parents to start nonjudgmentally noticing their internal experiences, including physical body sensations, thoughts, and emotions. Additionally, practitioners can help parents increase their awareness of external experiences, including actively noticing outside sensory experiences, listening to their child with full attention, and responding with emotional awareness. Table 1 outlines definitions and examples of these practices and presents methods early intervention practitioners can use to help parents strengthen these skills.

Proactive Strategies

Early intervention practitioners, such as Lisa, work with families to modify and adapt environments to promote a child's access to and participation in quality learning experiences. In much the same way, we recommend that practitioners who are working with families experiencing elevated stress should also consider proactive environmental arrangement strategies for parents. Here are a few examples of common mindfulness exercises that parents can try to rejuvenate and center themselves.

Deep breaths. Spending just a few minutes each day focusing on breathing can have cascading benefits throughout the day. Parents can do this while sitting on the floor, in a chair, or lying down. It can be helpful, in the beginning, to have parents place one hand on their belly and feel their abdomen rise on the inhale and fall on the exhale. Parents can pay attention to the temperature of the air as it enters and exits the nose. Practicing this skill in a proactive sense makes it easier for parents to draw upon at other times when it is needed for in-the-moment stress.

Body scan. Scanning one's body usually begins with attention placed on one part of the body, such as the forehead. Early intervention practitioners can teach parents to focus their attention and, as body sensations arise, notice and label them. For example, when placing attention on the forehead, the parent may notice an itch. If so, this may be labeled *itch*. If there is not a sensation that arises, that is okay too. Noticing the lack of sensation is also important. If no sensations arise, it may be helpful to guide attention back to their breathing. Next, parents scan the rest of their body. For example, the chest, right arm, left arm, stomach and back, and down each leg. This process can help parents relax their body and mind.

Stop and pause. Creating scheduled times throughout the day to stop, pause, and bring to mind an intention can be powerful. For example, it might be that a parent would like to be more patient with their child, or perhaps s/he has a goal of being more consistent with positive behavior supports. One way to achieve this is to set reminders or pleasant sounding bells, perhaps on a phone. When alerted, the parent will stop for two to three seconds and actively think about his or her intention. It is important for early intervention practitioners to remind parents to be nonjudgmental with themselves during this process. This is a time to actively bring to mind an intention, or family value, not judging "Am I

> Mindful parenting practices may help practitioners create supports for the parent to overcome this challenge while also aligning with the Family recommended practices on capacity building.

Table 1
Early Intervention Methods to Strengthen Mindful Parenting Skills and Capacity

Parent experiences	Definition and examples	Methods for practitioners
Noticing and describing internal experiences	Actively paying attention to internal experiences (i.e., body sensations, thoughts, and emotions) and describing them in words	• Ask parents to begin to notice their body and mind during different parent-child interactions. • Guide parents to become more aware of their sensations, thoughts, and emotions. It is important that this awareness be nonjudgmental. In other words, parents are not labeling their sensations, thoughts, and emotions as *good* or *bad* but rather simply noticing them and labeling them objectively.
Body sensations	Breathing, heart rate increasing and decreasing, tingling, itching, muscles tightening or loosening	• Support parents to bring a nonjudgmental awareness to body sensations. • Guide parents to notice and put into words different sensations they are feeling, or the lack of sensations. • Ask questions such as "What does that feel like?" "Where do you feel that stress in your body?" • Guide parents to notice their breathing, heart rate, and other sensations, such as muscle tension.
Thoughts	"Not this again," "We're going to be so late!" "I'm so glad that's over," "My child is trying so hard," "I'm so proud of her," "What am I going to cook for dinner?" "I need to make sure to send that e-mail"	• Help parents begin to notice their body sensations, then guide them to notice thoughts that are associated with those sensations. • Suggest parents label a thought as *thought* or *thinking*. This begins to allow them to observe their thoughts and see them for what they are—just thoughts. • Practice labeling thoughts in-the-moment, which can help parents be more present during parent-child interactions.
Emotions	Anxious, angry, exhausted, relieved, happy, excited	• Guide parents to describe in words their emotions when reflecting on routines. • Ask follow-up questions such as "What feeling were you having?" Sometimes this is best done after they have described their body sensations and thoughts.
Noticing and describing external experiences	Actively paying attention to outside sensations such as sounds, smells, shapes, colors, and light and describing them in words	• Guide parents to become more aware of their sensory system and how it influences everyday interactions with their child. • Ask open-ended questions such as "What sounds are you hearing?" or "What was the temperature like?" • Remind parents to label these outside sensations without adding a story or value to them.

Table 1 (continued)
Early Intervention Methods to Strengthen Mindful Parenting Skills and Capacity

Parent experiences	Definition and examples	Methods for practitioners
Listening with full attention	Parents focusing directly on their child, including verbal and nonverbal cues and facial expressions	• Provide question prompts to parents to lead them toward paying more attention to their child's language, social bids, and facial and body expressions.
Responding with emotional awareness	Noticing the internal states that surround body sensations and thought patterns and making a conscious decision to act with awareness instead of falling into automatic parenting cycles	• Prompt parents to pause and breathe when they are experiencing moments of parenting distress. This will increase the likelihood that they can respond to their child with intention instead of reverting to reactive patterns.

doing this enough?" or "Should I be better at this?"

Proactive strategies are not always going to be sufficient. It is inevitable that parents will also need to apply some in-the-moment mindful parenting strategies. In-the moment strategies can be used once parents notice and identify a stressful situation. In-the-moment strategies help parents recenter themselves after stress is heightened or be more aware of themselves and their child and avoid "checking out." Below are three different scenarios with suggestions of what Lisa might teach parents to address stressful situations.

Meredith's Stressful Evening

Meredith is a lawyer who works long hours. Her husband stays home with their 1-year-old, Sadie. When Meredith comes home from work, she is exhausted but wants quality time with Sadie. Meredith tries to make it home in time to put Sadie to bed, but she often feels that she cannot enjoy the time spent with her daughter because she is preoccupied with work stressors. Sadie often gets to bed late.

In-the moment suggestions for Meredith. Lisa suggests that Meredith practice labeling work-related thoughts as they arise when she is at home. This could help her be more present with her family and "turn off work," in a sense. When Meredith is spending quality time with Sadie and a thought pertaining to a work task she didn't finish or an e-mail she forgot to send arises, Lisa suggests that Meredith label that as *thought* or *planning*. Lisa tells Meredith that she does not need to push these thoughts away but rather just give them a label. Giving thoughts about past or future events a simple label can help parents detach a bit from them and be more present with their children.

Jorge's Morning Routine

Jorge is a young single father with two young children. Audrina is 2 years old, and Maria is 4 years old. Audrina attends the child care for employees of the factory where Jorge works full time. Maria has recently been diagnosed with autism spectrum disorder and has difficulty communicating her wants. Recently, she has been refusing to change into her school clothes and throws a tantrum

that includes dropping to the floor, screaming, and yelling "no, no, no" when Jorge asks her to get dressed. Mornings are becoming especially stressful for Jorge because he needs to drop off Maria across town and make it to the factory in time to drop off Audrina before his shift starts. As a result, Jorge has been written up twice for being late to work.

In-the-moment suggestions for Jorge. Lisa has already been working with Jorge and Maria to help Maria begin making choices by pointing to her clothing preferences. Lisa suggests that before Jorge enters Maria's room, he might take three deep breaths and notice any thoughts and emotions that arise. He will then be better able to know how his mood might affect Maria's behavior and be able to be more patient with Maria. If Maria begins to tantrum, before doing anything, Lisa suggests that Jorge take two to three slow, deep breaths and then try the choice-making strategy again.

Sandra's Dinnertime Routine

Sandra is Ricky's grandmother, and because his mother works late, Sandra picks him up from day care and feeds him dinner. Ricky is 5 years old and has developmental delays. Sandra often struggles during dinnertime, especially while she is trying to cook. Ricky often whines and cries or otherwise divides Sandra's attention while she is trying to prepare food. Sandra often resorts to putting Ricky in front of a television program or picking up fast food on the way home. Sandra wants to be able to use this time to teach Ricky about healthy eating and cooking.

In-the-moment suggestions for Sandra. Lisa is working with Sandra to help make Ricky more engaged during mealtime and even part of preparation when possible. For example, she has suggested that Sandra verbally label different foods (e.g., rice, chicken, carrots) and kitchen utensils and appliances (e.g., pot, oven, sink) as she is using them. To be more mindful with Ricky, Lisa has suggested that Sandra also label sensory experiences. For example, when cooking rice, first Sandra might say, "Rice is hard" and after it is finished cooking, she might say, "Rice is soft." Sandra can also describe different smells and sounds that arise as she is cooking. These strategies can help Ricky be more involved, receive the attention he needs, and perhaps learn some vocabulary along the way.

What Lisa's Learned . . .

Lisa has learned in her work with families that stressors connected to daily life impact parents' ability to use an intervention or strategy with their young child. By suggesting simple and brief mindful parenting practices, Lisa has helped families be more connected to each other and their surroundings during everyday routines. Lisa has found parents are more willing to try new techniques or use ones they have brainstormed together. She also knows that what works for one family will not work for all. She emphasizes to parents that the strategies they try need to easily fit into their existing routines, keeping in mind that the most important elements of mindful parenting are to be nonjudgmental and in the present moment with their child.

References

Bazzano A., Wolfe C., Zylovska L., Wang S., Schuster E., Barrett C., & Lehrer D. (2010). Stress-reduction and improved well-being following a pilot community-based participatory mindfulness-based stress-reduction (MBSR) program for parents/caregivers of children with developmental disabilities. *Disability and Health Journal, 3*, e6–e7. doi:10.1016/j.dhjo.2009.08.088

Beer, M., Ward, L., & Moar, K. (2013). The relationship between mindful parenting and distress in parents of children with autism spectrum disorder. *Mindfulness, 4*, 102–112. doi:10.1007/s12671-012-0192-4

Division for Early Childhood. (2014). *DEC recommended practices in early intervention/early childhood special education 2014.* Retrieved from http://www.dec-sped.org/recommendedpractices

Duncan, L. G., Coatsworth, J. D., & Greenberg, M. T. (2009). A model of mindful parenting: Implications for parent-child relationships and prevention research. *Clinical Child and Family Psychology Review, 12*, 255–270. doi:10.1007/s10567-009-0046-3

Jones, L., Hastings, R. P., Totsika, V., Keane, L., & Rhule, N. (2014). Child behavior problems and parental well-being in families of children with autism: The mediating role of mindfulness and acceptance. *American Journal on Intellectual and Developmental Disabilities, 119*, 171–185. doi:10.1352/1944-7558-119.2.171

Kabat-Zinn, M., & Kabat-Zinn, J. (1997). *Everyday blessings: The inner work of mindful parenting.* New York, NY: Hyperion.

Neece, C. L. (2014). Mindfulness-based stress reduction for parents of young children with developmental delays: Implications for parental mental health and child behavior problems. *Journal of Applied Research in Intellectual Disabilities, 27*, 174–186. doi:10.1111/jar.12064

Potharst, E. S., Aktar, E., Rexwinkel, M., Rigterink, M., & Bögels, S. M. (2017). Mindful with your baby: Feasibility, acceptability, and effects of a mindful parenting group training for mothers and their babies in a mental health context. *Mindfulness.* Advance online publication. doi:10.1007/s12671-017-0699-9

Reynolds, D. (2003). Mindful parenting: A group approach to enhancing reflective capacity in parents and infants. *Journal of Child Psychotherapy, 29*, 357–374. doi:10.1080/00754170310001625413

Singh, N. N., Lancioni, G. E., Winton, A. S. W., Fisher, B. C., Wahler, R. G., Mcaleavey, K., . . . Sabaawi, M. (2006). Mindful parenting decreases aggression, noncompliance, and self-injury in children with autism. *Journal of Emotional and Behavioral Disorders, 14*, 169–177. doi:10.1177/10634266060140030401

12

Putting It Together With You

Danielle M.
as told to Bonnie Keilty

What do [the Family] recommended practices mean? . . . One of the important pieces is, how do the recommended practices look for a family? Do families see [the recommended practices]? ... How can we make this language understandable for families? If one of the practices is speaking to developing plans, how are we really breaking that down for families? What does that look like for them? . . . Part of [applying] the practice is—the [practice itself] is well and good—how are we breaking down the application of the process so therapists better understand how to speak and work with families?

[For example], . . . you're given your rights at all these meetings. . . . It's six pages of [professionals saying], "These are your rights. So you have them now. Can you sign this paper that you have them? Okay, cool." And I feel that the rights hold no meaning. Can we explain these [Family recommended practices] to families in meetings? [For example], "This is what a therapist is working towards." . . . I'd like to have the therapist explain to me less formally and in more parent-friendly terms, "I have to do this assessment in six months." Or, "I'm looking for this." Or, "Let's develop these skills this way in your home. I know you have this many children and this schedule. Let's sit down and think about this. How could we really benefit your child?" EI is home based or family centered, but I think sometimes that gets lost. . . . Some of that family connection and the importance of that lens is lost among paperwork. I'm told to do activities, but they are not always realistic for me to work with my son on consistently. . . . Somebody always asks me your biggest concern, and I feel like you're talked at a lot. "This is your child's deficit, you know, X, Y, and Z." We're going to work on whatever therapeutic language and skills they come up with in their analysis, which is fine, that's their field. But how are we then taking that information and really working it back into the family? . . . There's a lot that goes on in the house; outside of the few minutes services are there. I think having a bigger picture for the service provider will be really helpful—where does this child fit into the family?

[Putting practices and procedures into family context] tends to become lost among the deficit language and data. . . . Our son goes to a center. So obviously they are unaware of the structure of my home or the dynamic of what is happening. . . . Some of the suggestions aren't realistic. They are simply not possible. And I, of course, want the best for my child, and I understand they're trying to help. However, at the same time, I think that they don't have enough of an understanding of what the house looks like. . . . Everybody's schedules are busy—parents are working, sometimes it's the nanny, and then you have two siblings that need to be taken places. [For example], I know my child needs to be doing tummy time, but I also have to take my other child to an activity and then go grocery shopping. . . . Thinking about the best practices around [those factors] would be really helpful.

I think for me, personally, [if there were initial conversations to understand the family and make sure strategies fit], I would have more of a game plan from the professionals. I think that this is a big part of my struggle. Yes, I know he needs to be doing X, Y, Z, but I don't necessarily know what that means inside of my house. Or I don't know what that means when we're doing this [routine]. So, I think having a variety [of] ideas in the toolbox and reevaluating them and saying "Okay, when we come to the six-month review, let's see how these strategies are working." Obviously, you can always discuss it with your therapist beforehand, but I think having specific, more realistic, suggestions for me makes it doable.

Because there can be many interventionists . . . there's a lot of chefs in the kitchen. And this therapist is telling me to do this, and this therapist is telling me to do this. Well, now what? I don't want to fail my child. Sometimes I have felt like a ping pong. So, I feel like if best practices are introduced and there's a way of therapists seeing themselves outside of their isolated fields, that would be helpful, in my opinion, for many families.

I think really building the foundation work within a family is huge. If [the relationship] starts off rough, everyone's attitudes have developed a certain way. The ambiguity can lead to misunderstandings or people not being able to do what they think is best. . . . I realize the therapists are all trying to give me their knowledge. Again, it comes back to the point of how therapists are collaborating to develop activities for "homework." Is there something I can do that pulls it all together as a family? . . . How are we navigating the dynamic of the family and putting these components together as therapists to really be family centered?

13

Prevent Teach Reinforce for Families
RESPECTing Families and Reducing Challenging Behaviors

JACLYN D. JOSEPH
PHILLIP S. STRAIN
ELIZABETH A. STEED
University of Colorado Denver

Nathan is 3 years old. He lives with his mother, father, and brother, who is 4 years old. Nathan's father travels for work, his mother works from home, and his brother attends preschool, so Nathan and his mother spend a significant amount of time together. Nathan's challenging behaviors are most apparent during the family's night and bedtime routine, and they also impact the family system. Nathan's father says, "Nathan has a severe case of the 'mommy's.' He refuses to let me do much of anything as long as his mom is around. Whether I'm super sweet and praise him, love on him, or scold him, it really doesn't matter. When mom is gone, he's like a totally different kid. He does what I ask, we have fun, and he even goes to bed and eats without issue most of the time." Nathan's mother indicates that if she wants to work during the evening hours (something she has to do because she works from home), she leaves the family home at bedtime so Nathan will not engage in challenging behaviors.

During a parent-teacher conference for Nathan's brother, his mother hears about a support the school provides to help families reduce challenging behaviors in the home. The process the school uses is called Prevent Teach Reinforce for Families (PTR-F; Dunlap et al., 2017). Nathan's mother schedules an initial meeting with a practitioner who uses PTR-F, and the family is eager, yet somewhat nervous, to begin working with the practitioner.

Introduction

Challenging behavior in young children (3 to 5 years of age) is a repeated pattern of behavior that interferes with the child's learning and/or development of social relationships (Powell, Fixsen, & Dunlap, 2003). Incidence studies suggest that the prevalence of persistent challenging behavior in the general preschool population is approximately 8–17% (Briggs-Gowan, Carter, Skuban, & Horwitz, 2001). When exhibited in the home setting, these challenging behaviors can disrupt a family routine, negatively impact interactions among family members, and put emotional and financial stress on the family system. This article will outline the particular struggles families of young children with challenging behaviors confront, followed by a description of seven characteristics of effective partnerships between families and practitioners. We will also illustrate how these partnership characteristics were applied with Nathan's family during an evidence-based and collaborative process of family-centered positive behavior support to reduce challenging behavior in their home.

Unique Challenges Presented by Families Experiencing Challenging Behavior

Challenging behavior, it is said, is powerful behavior, especially powerful in its range and breadth of impact. Specifically, challenging behavior can elicit strong emotions, negatively impact family quality of life, and result in adult disputes

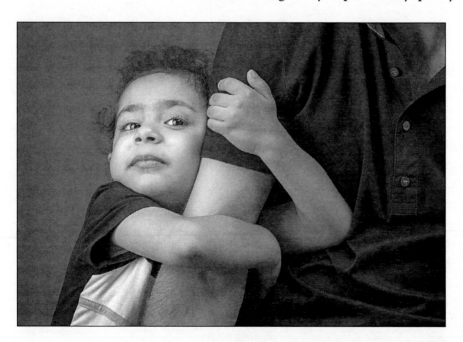

about what is challenging in the first place and what practices to use to address the behaviors. These "challenges" are further compounded by the ubiquitous nature of parenting advice and the predictable confusion and frustration this causes for adult family members.

Challenging behavior is upsetting. In many families, child challenging behaviors can lead to strong emotional responses by adults. Adult family members can and do feel inadequate, angry, and frustrated. Moreover, these feelings can and do spill over into blaming, shaming, and related frustrations among adult family members. For practitioners of support, it is essential to understand that helping adults manage their emotional responses may be just as vital to reducing child challenging behaviors as changing patterns of parent-child interactions. While most practitioners of positive behavior support are perfectly comfortable with providing direction and help around parent-child interactions, adult family members who are overwhelmed with emotions are, in the moment, not the best candidates for skill training and support. Therefore, practitioners of instrumental support also need to be comfortable and competent in delivering emotional support.

Challenging behavior already can have negatively impacted family

quality of life. It is very common for families to have made major changes to their routines and parenting practices in an effort to prevent episodes of problem behavior. Often referred to as "coercive family processes," we see families eating at fast food restaurants daily to avoid the prospect of their child tantruming about food choices, families not leaving the house to avoid public displays of child aggressive behavior, and families allowing hours of nightly TV viewing in hopes of staving off a battle over the time for bed (Patterson, 1982). Over time, we know that these behavior patterns only increase the likelihood of future challenges and that they can result in an increased incidence in adult depression and insularity from community supports (Strain & Timm, 2001). For practitioners, it is essential to consider these family concerns as important targets for support.

There is a high probability of disagreement about what challenging behavior is. We often say that the "real" definition of challenging behavior is behavior that is disturbing to adults that adults want to see stopped. This definition, in fact, reflects an essential truth that adult family members and practitioners often have very different views about what behaviors are "challenging." Obviously, differing views about challenging behaviors directly impact the focus of intervention efforts themselves, but they also impact how families and practitioners interpret success. For some families, reducing tantrums from one hour to five minutes is a very desirable outcome. For others, five minutes is still way too stressful. The challenge for practitioners is keeping their definitions out of the way and understanding that "success" is always going to be defined in a unique way by each family.

Parenting advice is everywhere. Many of the former families with whom we have worked have spent a great deal of time and resources trying to find the best ways to prevent continuing episodes of challenging behaviors. Families have relied on relatives, teachers, the Internet, popular press books, TV experts, and private practice clinicians. Perhaps it is not too much of an exaggeration to claim that parenting experts are everywhere and most everyone is ready with advice. As a consequence, many families have strong views about how they should be interacting with their child, and many have deep commitments to historically ineffective practices. The challenge for practitioners then is not just equipping adult family members with a set of skills but also supporting them in stopping a set of practices!

> Challenging behaviors can disrupt a family routine, negatively impact interactions among family members, and put emotional and financial stress on the family system.

RESPECTing Families

To help families reduce challenging behaviors at home, we use a manualized model of individualized positive behavior support (Prevent Teach Reinforce for Families, or PTR-F). PTR-F has five steps (initiating the process, assessment, intervention, coaching, and monitoring plan implementation and child progress), and across each step of the process, we have developed the acronym RESPECT to symbolize some of the key practices that family-practitioner partnerships require. The partnership practices represented in RESPECT are Reciprocal exchange, Enhance quality of life, Systemic perspective, Progress monitoring, Evidence-based practices, Contextual fit, and Teaming. These RESPECT practices are not only applicable for practitioners using the PTR-F process, though. We believe that any family-practitioner partnership would be greatly enhanced by these practices, each of which is described and illustrated next.

Reciprocal Exchange

In reciprocal exchanges, the expertise of both families and professionals is valued (Fettig, Schultz, & Ostrosky, 2013; Lucyshyn, Horner, Dunlap, Albin, & Ben, 2002). Reciprocal exchange not only refers to the sharing of information and the active participation of families in the development and implementation of interventions, it also refers to specific behaviors that should occur (Brookman-Frazee & Koegel, 2004; Carr, Dunlap, et al., 2002; McLaughlin, Denney, Snyder, & Welsh, 2012).

When working to reduce challenging behavior, progress can be slow and hard to feel, so it is important for families and practitioners to have an ongoing, visual representation of the magnitude of the challenging behavior over time.

Reciprocal exchanges occurred frequently between Nathan's parents and the practitioner to collaboratively find a solution to Nathan's challenging behavior. The practitioner provided the family with information about how the PTR-F process would work. During the assessment process, Nathan's family and the practitioner met to exchange information about behavior that was most troubling to the family during the bedtime routine. Nathan's family and the practitioner discussed what was happening during this routine to ensure their mutual understanding of the situation.

During Steps 1 through 3, Nathan's family and the practitioner collaborated to identify the target behavior. Nathan's family chose "following the bedtime routine" and, with the practitioner, defined this target as "using a quiet voice" and "following the steps of the parent-defined bedtime routine (with prompting) without demonstrating challenging behavior." The family and practitioner discussed various prevent and teaching strategies to use to meet this target behavior. They agreed on three prevent strategies (enhance predictability with calendars and schedules, reduce distractions or competing events or materials, and use scripted social stories to describe problematic situations and potential solutions); one teaching strategy (teach independence with visual schedules and calendars); and many reinforce strategies to best address the challenging behaviors and work for Nathan's family.

Enhance Quality of Life

The goal of working with families around challenging behavior is to ultimately create durable changes in the family system (Buschbacher, Fox, & Clarke, 2004). Skills are strategically transferred to members of the child's family so they will eventually be able to problem-solve difficulties without requiring the direct support of practitioners (Harrower, Fox, Dunlap, & Kincaid, 2000). Therefore, families are able to maintain lifestyle changes that work to prevent and target future occurrences of challenging behavior and promote continued positive outcomes as children develop (Buschbacher et al., 2004; Harrower et al., 2000).

Nathan's family and the practitioner met to discuss and define desirable behaviors to encourage during the bedtime routine. These behaviors were specifically selected to make the bedtime routine better for the family. Nathan's family wanted Nathan's dad to be able to "do the bedtime routine" without Nathan "engaging in tantruming behavior."

One of the tools the practitioner used when helping Nathan's parents implement the behavior plan was coaching. Coaching was used to transfer skills to Nathan's family so they would be able to independently implement the behavioral support plan (BSP) and solve difficulties in the future without the practitioner so they could enjoy the quality of life they desired.

Systemic Perspective

The family system is frequently cited as the most influential and important learning context for young children (Barton & Fettig, 2013; Dunst, Trivette, & Hamby, 2008; Powell & Dunlap, 2010). Practitioners work collaboratively with family members to determine supports that can be provided for children during daily routines that are practical and easily performed and that result in more successful routines (Marshall & Mirenda, 2002). Therefore, practitioners partnering with families to reduce challenging behaviors perform essential tasks (i.e., functional assessment, behavior support plan [BSP] implementation) with families when the routine occurs (Harrower et al., 2000).

The systemic perspective was helpful for Nathan's parents and the practitioner to look at how Nathan's challenging behaviors occurred. Nathan's family and the practitioner talked about how sometimes, but not always, the bedtime routine differed depending on which parent did the routine. If Nathan's father completed the routine with him while his mother was not home, Nathan would often fall asleep on his own without his father in his room. This rarely happened if his mother was home. Together they considered the family system and how various routines occurred to gain a comprehensive picture of the family's life and particularly of Nathan's challenging behavior.

Progress Monitoring

When working to reduce challenging behavior, progress can be slow and hard to feel, so it is important for families and practitioners to have an ongoing, visual representation of the magnitude of the challenging behavior over time. It is just as important for families and practitioners to have an objective understanding of how the family's behavior has changed over time. Family-practitioner partnerships should continuously evaluate the child's progress and ensure that the

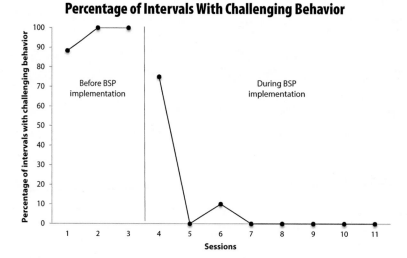

Figure 1

Percentage of Challenging Behavior During Bedtime Routine for Nathan Across Sessions

> Families of young children are diverse, and practitioners need to consider the cultural responsiveness of practices when assessing the contextual fit of the family-centered positive behavior support approach.

plan is being implemented by adult family members as intended to promote the likelihood that the family will meet their goals (Harrower et al., 2000; Marshall & Mirenda, 2002).

Nathan's parents and the practitioner developed a monitoring process that would allow both parents and practitioner to determine whether the BSP was being implemented effectively and whether Nathan's behavior was improving. As seen in Figure 1, when Nathan's parents started the process, Nathan exhibited challenging behaviors during 96% of the family's bedtime routines. By the fifth week of partnering, Nathan's family noted a dramatic decrease in his challenging behaviors. After 11 weeks, Nathan's challenging behaviors were no longer occurring at bedtime.

Evidence-based Practices

Another way to RESPECT families is to support them in the implementation of evidence-based practices. Partnering with families to reduce challenging behavior involves a variety of evidence-based practices including, but not limited to, monitoring progress and making data-based decisions; engaging in functional assessment; providing practice-based coaching; and developing comprehensive BSPs that include research-validated antecedent, instructional, and reinforcement strategies.

The strategies identified in reciprocal exchange between Nathan's family and the practitioner were all evidence-based practices. These included the prevent strategies of enhancing predictability with calendars and schedules, reducing distractions or competing events or materials, and using scripted social stories to describe problematic situations and potential solutions. They also included the teaching strategy of teaching independence with visual schedules and calendars and many reinforcement strategies.

After the initial BSP implementation, everyone agreed that the family needed some more support with implementing the BSP. A meeting was scheduled with Nathan's mother and father to review the BSP and ensure that the strategies still fit well into the family's ecology. Role playing and coaching were used to ensure that both parents felt confident and able to implement the BSP. The goal of coaching, an evidence-based practice, was to transfer skills to Nathan's family so they would be able to independently implement the BSP.

Contextual Fit

Through collaborative family-practitioner partnerships and family-centered practices, BSPs can have a good contextual fit with families (Harrower et al., 2000; McLaughlin et al., 2012; Moes & Frea, 2002). Contextual fit refers to how much the BSP fits into the family's life as well as the BSP's ability to effectively meet their needs (McLaughlin et al., 2012; Moes & Frea, 2002). BSPs that fit well into a family's ecology are more likely to be implemented consistently with fidelity and to be generalized (McLaughlin et al., 2012). Family ecology refers to concepts such as values, parenting practices, and resources, and it illuminates a significant concern of contextual fit (McLaughlin et al., 2012). Families of young children are diverse, and practitioners need to consider the cultural responsiveness of practices when assessing the contextual fit of

the family-centered positive behavior support (PBS) approach. Cultural responsiveness includes the process (i.e., how practitioners interact and communicate with families) and the products (i.e., BSPs) that comprise an approach.

After discussing the family's values and parenting practices, the family and practitioner concluded that Nathan could learn to request his wants and needs, express emotions and aversions, and express preferences when given a choice. His family also identified social skills such as getting attention appropriately, sharing, taking turns, and waiting for acknowledgment or reinforcement that, if taught to Nathan, could reduce challenging behavior. Further, Nathan's mother and father identified a number of problem-solving skills that, if learned, could reduce the likelihood of the challenging behavior in the future. Nathan's parents took the lead in these decisions, which ensured that the social skills and problem-solving skills were appropriate for their family.

Teaming

Different from expert- or professional-driven models, partnerships should involve active participation of families in the development and implementation of interventions (Brookman-Frazee & Koegel, 2004; Carr, Dunlap, et al., 2002; McLaughlin et al., 2012). Research has shown that when families are actively involved, the likelihood that interventions will be successful increases (Carr, Horner, et al., 1999; Powell, Dunlap, & Fox, 2006). Both families and professionals are considered to have expertise that is valuable and necessary (Fettig et al., 2013).

Nathan's family and the practitioner met for about an hour and a half to develop the BSP. They engaged in reciprocal exchanges to review, choose, and plan for the intervention strategies that would be used in Nathan's BSP. Conversations ensured the family could use each strategy in the BSP during Nathan's bedtime routine and that they believed the strategies would meet their needs.

Even though Nathan's father could not attend all the meetings, Nathan's mother updated her husband after each meeting so that he continued to be part of the team. She shared his thoughts with the practitioner. The practitioner was available to respond to any questions the father might have.

Conclusion

In this example, the practitioner and Nathan's family worked collaboratively to implement a BSP with prevent, teach, and reinforcement strategies to reduce Nathan's challenging behavior during bedtime. The RESPECT practices outlined in this paper offer even greater potential to enhance family-practitioner partnerships while developing clear behavioral goals and implementing assessment, intervention, coaching, and progress monitoring to provide lasting benefits to families and children. RESPECTful collaboration is key so families are positioned to carry out interventions themselves with competence and confidence.

References

Barton, E. E., & Fettig, A. (2013). Parent-implemented interventions for young children with disabilities: A review of fidelity features. *Journal of Early Intervention, 35,* 194–219. doi:10.1177/1053815113504625

Briggs-Gowan, M. J., Carter, A. S., Skuban, E. M., & Horwitz, S. M. (2001). Prevalence of social-emotional and behavioral problems in a community sample of 1- and 2-year-old children. *Journal of the American Academy of Child and Adolescent Psychiatry, 40,* 811–819. doi:10.1097/00004583-200107000-00016

Brookman-Frazee, L., & Koegel, R. L. (2004). Using parent/clinician partnerships in parent education programs for children with autism. *Journal of Positive Behavior Interventions, 6,* 195–213. doi:10.1177/10983007040060040201

Buschbacher, P., Fox, L., & Clarke, S. (2004). Recapturing desired family routines: A parent professional behavioral collaboration. *Research and Practice for Persons with Severe Disabilities, 29,* 25–39. doi:10.2511/rpsd.29.1.25

Carr, E. G., Dunlap, G., Horner, R. H., Koegel, R. L., Turnbull, A. P., Sailor, W., . . . Fox, L. (2002). Positive behavior support: Evolution of an applied science. *Journal of Positive Behavior Interventions, 4,* 4–16. doi:10.1177/109830070200400102

Carr, E. G., Horner, R. H., Turnbull, A. P., Marquis, J. G., McLaughlin, D. M., McAtee, M. L., . . . Doolabh, A. (1999). *Positive behavior support for people with developmental disabilities: A research synthesis.* Washington, DC: American Association on Mental Retardation.

Dunlap, G., Strain, P. S., Lee, J., K., Joseph, J. D., Vatland, C., & Fox, L. (2017). *Prevent-teach-reinforce for families: A model of individualized positive behavior support for home and community.* Baltimore, MD: Paul H. Brookes.

Dunst, C. J., Trivette, C. M., & Hamby, D. W. (2008). *Research synthesis and meta-analysis of studies of family-centered practices.* Asheville, NC: Winterberry Press.

Fettig, A., Schultz, T. R., & Ostrosky, M. M. (2013). Collaborating with parents in using effective strategies to reduce children's challenging behaviors. *Young Exceptional Children, 16*(1), 30–41. doi:10.1177/1096250612473127

Harrower, J. K., Fox, L., Dunlap, G., & Kincaid, D. (2000). Functional assessment and comprehensive early intervention. *Exceptionality: A Special Education Journal, 8,* 189–204. doi:10.1207/s15327035ex0803_5

Lucyshyn, J. M., Horner, R. H., Dunlap, G., Albin, R. W., & Ben, K. R. (2002). Positive behavior support with families. In J. M. Lucyshyn, G. Dunlap, & R. W. Albin (Eds.), *Families and positive behavior support: Addressing problem behavior in family contexts* (pp. 3—43). Baltimore, MD: Paul H. Brookes.

Marshall, J. K., & Mirenda, P. (2002). Parent-professional collaboration for positive behavior support in the home. *Focus on Autism and Other Developmental Disabilities, 17,* 216–228. doi:10.1177/10883576020170040401

McLaughlin, T. W., Denney, M. K., Snyder, P. A., & Welsh, J. L. (2012). Behavior support interventions implemented by families of young children: Examination of contextual fit. *Journal of Positive Behavior Interventions, 14,* 87–97. doi:10.1177/1098300711411305

Moes, D. R., & Frea, W. D. (2002). Contextualized behavioral support in early intervention for children with autism and their families. *Journal of Autism and Developmental Disorders, 32,* 519–533. doi:10.1023/A:1021298729297

Patterson, G. R. (1982). *Coercive family process.* Eugene, OR: Castalia.

Powell, D., & Dunlap, G. (2010, September). *Family-focused interventions for promoting social-emotional development in infants and toddlers with or at risk for disabilities* (Roadmap to Effective Intervention Practices No. 5). Tampa: University of South Florida, Technical Assistance Center on Social Emotional Intervention for Young Children.

Powell, D., Dunlap, G., & Fox, L. (2006). Prevention and intervention for the challenging behaviors of toddlers and preschoolers. *Infants & Young Children, 19,* 25–35.

Powell, D., Fixsen, D., & Dunlap, G. (2003, May 30). *Pathways to service utilization: A synthesis of evidence relevant to young children with challenging behavior.* Tampa: University of South Florida, Center for Evidence-Based Practice: Young Children with Challenging Behaviors.

Strain, P. S., & Timm, M. A. (2001). Remediation and prevention of aggression: An evaluation of the Regional Intervention Program over a quarter century. *Behavioral Disorders, 26,* 297–313.

14

Families as Mentors
A Model for Preparing Practitioners to Engage in Family-Centered Practices

Ariane N. Gauvreau
Susan R. Sandall
University of Washington

Ensuring early childhood teachers are adequately prepared to partner with and support families is a goal for all teacher preparation programs. Family involvement and support are critical components of effective special education programs (Division for Early Childhood, 2014; National Association for the Education of Young Children, 2005). Early childhood teachers must be able to develop meaningful relationships with families and engage in family-centered practices. Family-centered practices refer to a practitioner's ability to develop a reciprocal, respectful partnership to provide effective services to children and families that strengthen family functioning (Dunst & Espe-Sherwindt, 2016; Dunst, Trivette, & Hamby, 2007). As our population becomes increasingly diverse, it is equally important that practitioners be sufficiently prepared to support families from cultural, ethnic, linguistic, and socioeconomic backgrounds different from their own. As Fults and Harry (2012) note, "in a multicultural world, it is not possible to be family centered without being culturally responsive" (p. 28).

This paper focuses on methods for preparing teachers for early intervention (birth to age 3) and early childhood special education, including those teachers in blended programs. We refer to the individuals learning to be teachers as preservice teachers. The purpose of this article is to describe the issues around preparation of teachers to understand and implement family-centered practices.

Personnel Preparation and the DEC Recommended Practices

The DEC Recommended Practices (2014) in the Family topic area encompass three main concepts that all ECSE personnel should apply: family-centered practices, family capacity building practices, and family collaboration. These practices propose that EI/ECSE personnel encourage active participation of family members in decisions and meaningful family involvement in the service plan and also support families in developing and achieving goals that will promote the well-being of their child with a disability as well as their family. Upon close examination of the recommended practices, it is evident that these skills and behaviors are applied skills that EI/ECSE practitioners demonstrate with families. Applied knowledge and skills provide a unique challenge for personnel preparation programs because they are not easily taught or assessed through coursework alone. Coursework provides the foundational and theoretical knowledge of why these practices are important, but it's within field experiences that preservice teachers actually observe and engage in these practices. While fieldwork is a requirement of most teacher preparation programs (Hammerness, Darling-Hammond, Grossman, Rust, & Shulman, 2005), targeted field experiences involving the families of young children with disabilities are crucial in the instruction and enactment of these practices.

The Importance of Family Involvement in ECSE

It is well documented that beginning teachers are challenged by how to effectively engage and collaborate with families (Able, Ghulamani, Mallous, & Glazier, 2014; Bruder, Dunst, Wilson, & Stayton, 2013; Pretti-Frontczak, Giallourakis, Janas, & Hayes, 2002), especially those from cultural and linguistic backgrounds different from their own (Sewell, 2012). Yet, early childhood programs with high levels of family engagement, communication, and social support are associated with better parent outcomes, including increased involvement with their children, greater feelings of self-efficacy, and better understanding of child development (El Nokali, Bachman, & Votruba-Drzal, 2010; Marcon, 1999). Given the positive outcomes associated with programs that have high levels of family involvement, ensuring that all early childhood special educators are sufficiently prepared to engage in family-centered practices is imperative. Yet, how to best prepare teachers for this important aspect of their work is still unknown.

Traditional Coursework Is Not Enough

While there is limited research on how personnel preparation can best address family-centered practices, the field of early childhood special education has focused on two main concepts: the importance of opportunities to engage with families in fieldwork (Able et al., 2014; Capone & DiVenere, 1996; Mandell & Murray, 2005) and questions about the effectiveness of stand-alone courses (Fults & Harry, 2012; McBride, Sharp, Hains, & Whitehead, 1995).

Field experiences emphasizing family-centered practices or settings with a high level of family involvement were effective in influencing the beliefs and attitudes of preservice teachers (Able et al., 2014; Mandell & Murray, 2005). Conversely, while coursework addressing family partnerships is an important part of the pedagogy, it may not be enough to impact preservice teachers' beliefs or adequately prepare them to partner with families once they enter the classroom

> Given the positive outcomes associated with programs that have high levels of family involvement, ensuring that all early childhood special educators are sufficiently prepared to engage in family-centered practices is imperative.

(Bingham & Abernathy, 2007; McCollum, Rowan, & Thorpe, 1994; Sewell, 2012).

While coursework addresses the foundational theories and background information necessary to understand the importance of and methods for collaboration with families, traditional coursework alone does not provide sufficient opportunity for preservice teachers to adopt these notions into their personal belief system or enact these practices (Capone & DiVenere, 1996). However, courses that include assignments requiring students to engage with families through interviews or observations are effective in shaping beliefs and practices toward becoming more family centered (Capone, Hull, & DiVenere, 1997; Fults & Harry, 2012) and are one way programs can ensure that teachers have authentic opportunities to interact with families and are prepared to engage in family-centered practices in the future.

Parents as Coinstructors

Some personnel preparation programs have collaborated with families as coinstructors (Capone et al., 1997; McBride et al., 1995). While a faculty instructor may use lectures or case studies to illustrate the complexity of supporting a family through the special education referral process, it is arguably more powerful for

students to hear about this process from a parent and learn about their personal experiences, including the emotions, the need for information, the questions, and the complex life experiences entwined in this process (McBride et al., 1995). However, this model may not be sustainable for all personnel preparation programs because it requires specific resources, including identification and recruitment of family members who have the time and resources to participate in course development, planning, grading, and lecturing. It also affords the perspective of just one parent. Other course-related enhancements,  such as reading books by parent authors, parent panels, and so forth, may aid students' knowledge of families and family life but have little impact on actual practice.

Fieldwork

Field experiences include the "authentic contexts in which preservice teachers can apply the theory of teaching" (O'Brian, Stoner, Appel, & House, 2007) and are one of the most influential components of a teacher's preparation program (Potthoff & Alley, 1996). Through field experiences (also called *practicum, student teaching, internships,* and *fieldwork*), preservice teachers make important course-to-field connections, observe a skilled mentor engaging in effective practices, engage and collaborate with other practitioners, and implement instructional strategies they have learned in coursework (Aiken & Day, 1999; Feiman-Nemser, 2001; O'Brian et al., 2007). However, given that many practicing teachers report feeling unprepared to support families (Able et al., 2014; Bruder et al., 2013; Pretti-Frontczak et al., 2002), it is possible that preservice teachers may not be observing high-quality family-centered practices within these placements. Therefore, these programs may consider alternatives that specifically target family partnerships and family-centered practices.

Targeting Family-Centered Practices Through Field Experiences: The Families as Mentors Program

The Families as Mentors Program is one method used in the University of Washington's dual endorsement, graduate teacher preparation program. The Families as Mentors Program builds on the early description of Capone et al. (1997)

and represents numerous iterations to fit our context. An essential feature of this program is that families serve as mentors and experienced and knowledgeable guides. Family mentors are recruited through our partnerships with birth to age 3 centers, preschools, and early elementary classrooms in our area. We try to recruit mentors from various backgrounds, ensuring students can engage with same-sex parents, families who speak languages other than English, families involved with the foster care system, families with multiple children with disabilities, families with single parents, families who have immigrated from other countries, and families of various socioeconomic statuses.

All preservice teachers are paired with a family who has a child with a disability and accompany families on their daily activities for several months. A main goal is for preservice teachers to gain insight into the routine successes and challenges these families experience. Common activities include making a trip to the grocery store, attending a school meeting (e.g., IEP, IFSP, home visit), or spending time in the community. At minimum, students are required to meet with their family five times across an academic year. This project is frequently discussed in our practicum seminar and referenced in other courses, providing students with an opportunity to share their experience, problem solve (e.g., scheduling, how to reach out to unresponsive families), and learn about the experiences of their peers, including a greater range of experiences with families from various cultural, linguistic, and ethnic backgrounds.

This project is in addition to four required practicum placements (two ECSE placements, one early childhood general education placement, and one yearlong student teaching placement) and two courses on families and communities. By seeing different sides of the educational system (a family's perspective and several birth to age 8 education settings), we hope our graduates enter the teaching profession with a deep understanding of how the educational system can better meet the needs of diverse families.

Results of an Initial Study

A recent study involving both preservice teachers and family mentors suggested that this program and experience is useful, informative, and valuable for all parties involved. Data were collected through online surveys distributed to both preservice teachers and family mentors. Preservice teachers were asked about their beliefs, experiences, and challenges with this project through open-ended questions. Family mentors were asked about their experience as a mentor, their confidence in their mentee to engage in family-centered practices, and their impressions of their mentee through Likert-scale items and open-ended questions. The response rate was 100% for preservice teachers and 80% for family mentors.

Preservice teachers. Several main themes emerged from data from preservice teachers. Themes were:

> Many preservice teachers expressed shock at how busy families were and acknowledged that raising children, advocating for services, managing full-time jobs, appointments, school, etc., requires an exceptional amount of work.

- An overall greater understanding of families with children with disabilities and children with disabilities outside the school or early intervention context
- Increased clarity of how to transfer theory to practice
- Ideas for how to better accommodate families in the future
- A better understanding of services from a family perspective.

All preservice teachers seemed to think differently about families after completion of this project. In addition to observing the struggles, celebrations, and challenges that families with young children with disabilities experience daily, they also were able to better understand our current educational, social service, and health systems and how these systems may both support and alienate individuals with disabilities and their families. Many preservice teachers expressed shock at how busy families were and acknowledged that raising children, advocating for services, managing full-time jobs, appointments, school, etc., requires an exceptional amount of work.

One preservice teacher described accompanying her family mentor to a dental appointment and observing the parent debating a certain procedure with the dentist, then ultimately declining this service.

> I was so surprised to see the mother advocate for her son at his dentist appointment. The dentist insisted that her child go through a certain procedure, but she insisted that he was wrong and ended up making a different choice. She knew what was best for him.

Another preservice teacher spent time with her family mentor at a community-based outdoor camp for children with disabilities and met other families of young children. She reflected on their perspectives of certain local services, expressing surprise that the family was not satisfied with what was available.

> My mentor family and many others expressed a great deal of displeasure with services provided in the area, including some specific ones that surprised me more than others. I'm surprised and feel challenged by some of the stories they've shared about their experiences, and it was incredibly helpful to hear their perspectives.

Understanding a family's personal experience with the educational services and extracurricular activities available to young children with disabilities is a crucial component in preparing teachers to be critical consumers of services designed to support families.

Understanding a family's personal experience with the educational services and extracurricular activities available to young children with disabilities is a crucial component in preparing teachers to be critical consumers of services designed to support families. Personal recommendations from families such as this one may be useful resources as these teachers embark on their careers in this area, enabling them to provide more meaningful information to the families they will serve in the future.

Several respondents discussed their newfound understanding of how challenging life can be for families. One respondent reflected: "You can't just move on and there isn't a pause button. If a child has a meltdown in public, you don't get to send them on the bus home, you have to have this insane amount of longevity." Another noted the contrast in the child's behavior between school and home, commenting: "I got to see the ways her disability did impact her, and getting closer to her family showed me that it impacted her in ways I wouldn't have guessed." When asked about what surprised them, one student reflected on collaboration: "It reminded me that collaboration with families doesn't mean me listening to them and telling me what they need, but can also be them sharing things with me that I didn't know about before."

A significant take away for many was the practicality of certain interventions within a family's routine.

> This project helped me put our interventions into a more meaningful context. Seeing how my mentor family adapted interventions for the chaos of daily life helped me understand why information for families and plans for children need to be accessible, and in as much plain language as possible.

Thus, data suggest this project influenced the way preservice teachers understood implementation of recommended practices in the home, viewed families as advocates for their children, and shifted their thinking around the knowledge to be shared and gained between teachers and families.

Family mentors. Family mentors reported positive experiences as well. All mentors reported feeling "very confident" in their mentee's ability to engage in family-centered practices in the future and felt it is "very important" for preservice teachers to spend time learning from families. When asked what they think their mentee learned from their family, mentors shared "that families with

special needs children face a plethora of obstacles while navigating the 'system.' "
Another mentor shared that this was a "great opportunity for us both. . . . The
home environment is very different from therapy and school time. [This proj-
ect] gives a better picture overall." Someone else hoped their mentee learned
the complexities of having a child with a disability and how this can impact all
aspects of a family's life, in and outside of school. Lastly, all mentors shared that
their student was respectful, open-minded, and willing to learn from their family.

Results from this study suggest that authentic, hands-on opportunities may
be more effective in facilitating family-centered beliefs and practices than traditional courses and fieldwork alone, consistent with other studies demonstrating
that hands-on experiences are more influential than coursework alone (Able
et al., 2014; Jordan, Schwartz, & McGhie-Richmond, 2009).

Implications for Personnel Preparation Programs

All programs preparing early childhood personnel must focus on family-centered practices. Yet, traditional coursework is not adequately preparing teachers
to effectively partner with the range of
families receiving special education and
early intervention services (Bingham &
Abernathy, 2007; McCollum et al., 1994;
Sewell, 2012). While involving parents
in traditional coursework through parent panels and coteaching is one way to
embed the perspective of families (Mc-
Bride et al., 1995), hands-on opportunities
may be more powerful in supporting
teachers to use family-centered practices.
The results of this study, consistent with
other literature (Able et al., 2014), suggest
that including an authentic opportunity
for preservice teachers to engage with
families in their natural environments is
a crucial aspect of personnel preparation

in early childhood special education. By ensuring more special educators enter
the field prepared and eager to partner with families, we are ensuring better
long-term outcomes for children, families, communities, and schools.

References

Able, H., Ghulamani, H., Mallous, R., & Glazier, J. (2014). Service learning: A
promising strategy for connecting future teachers to the lives of diverse children and their families. *Journal of Early Childhood Teacher Education*, 35,
6–21. doi:10.1080/10901027.2013.874383
Aiken, I. P., & Day, B. D. (1999). Early field experiences in preservice teacher
education: Research and student perspectives. *Action in Teacher Education*,
21(3), 7–12. doi:10.1080/01626620.1999.10462965

Bingham, A., & Abernathy, T. V. (2007). Promoting family-centered teaching: Can one course make a difference? *Issues in Teacher Education, 16*(1), 37–60.

Bruder, M. B., Dunst, C. J., Wilson, C., & Stayton, V. (2013). Predictors of confidence and competence among early childhood interventionists. *Journal of Early Childhood Teacher Education, 34,* 249–267. doi:10.1080/10901027.2013.816806

Capone, A. M., & DiVenere, N. (1996). The evolution of a personnel preparation program: Preparation of family-centered practitioners. *Journal of Early Intervention, 20,* 222–231. doi:10.1177/105381519602000306

Capone, A., Hull, K. M., & DiVenere, N. J. (1997). Parent-professional partnerships in preservice and inservice education. In P. J. Winton, J. A. McCollum, & C. Catlett (Eds.), *Reforming personnel preparation in early childhood education: Issues, models, and practical strategies* (pp. 435–453). Baltimore, MD: Paul H. Brookes.

Division for Early Childhood. (2014). *DEC recommended practices in early intervention/early childhood special education 2014.* Retrieved from http://www.dec-sped.org/recommendedpractices

Dunst, C. J., & Espe-Sherwindt, M. (2016). Family-centered practices in early childhood intervention. In B. Reichbow, B. A. Boyd, E. E. Barton, & S. L. Odom (Eds.), *Handbook of early childhood special education* (pp. 37–55). Cham, Switzerland: Springer.

Dunst, C. J., Trivette, C. M., & Hamby, D. W. (2007). Meta-analysis of family-centered helpgiving practices research. *Mental Retardation and Developmental Disabilities Research Reviews, 13,* 370–378. doi:10.1002/mrdd.20176

El Nokali, N. E., Bachman, H. J., & Votruba-Drzal, E. (2010). Parent involvement and children's academic and social development in elementary school. *Child Development, 81,* 988–1005. doi:10.1111/j.1467-8624.2010.01447.x

Feiman-Nemser, S. (2001). From preparation to practice: Designing a continuum to strengthen and sustain teaching. *Teachers College Record, 103,* 1013–1055.

Fults, R. M., & Harry, B. (2012). Combining family centeredness and diversity in early childhood teacher training programs. *Teacher Education and Special Education, 35,* 27–48. doi:10.1177/0888406411399784

Hammerness, K., Darling-Hammond, L., Grossman, P., Rust, F., & Shulman, L. (2005). The design of teacher education programs. In L. Darling-Hammond & J. Bransford (Eds.), *Preparing teachers for a changing world: What teachers should learn and be able to do* (pp. 390–441). San Francisco, CA: Jossey-Bass.

Jordan, A., Schwartz, E., & McGhie-Richmond, D. (2009). Preparing teachers for inclusive classrooms. *Teaching and Teacher Education, 25,* 535–542. doi:10.1016/j.tate.2009.02.010

Mandell, C. J., & Murray, M. M. (2005). Innovative family-centered practices in personnel preparation. *Teacher Education and Special Education, 28,* 74–77. doi:10.1177/088840640502800108

Marcon, R. A. (1999). Positive relationships between parent school involvement and public school inner-city preschoolers' development and academic performance. *School Psychology Review, 28,* 395–412.

McBride, S. L., Sharp, L., Hains, A. H., & Whitehead, A. (1995). Parents as co-instructors in preservice training: A pathway to family-centered practice. *Journal of Early Intervention, 19,* 343–355. doi:10.1177/105381519501900408

McCollum, J. A., Rowan, L. R., & Thorp, E. K. (1994). Philosophy as training in infancy personnel preparation. *Journal of Early Intervention, 18,* 216–226. doi:10.1177/105381519401800208

National Association for the Education of Young Children. (2005). *NAEYC early childhood program standards.* Washington, DC: Author. Retrieved from http://www.naeyc.org/files/naeyc/Position%20Statement%20EC%20Standards.pdf

O'Brian, M., Stoner, J., Appel, K., & House, J. J. (2007). The first field experience: Perspectives of preservice and cooperating teachers. *Teacher Education and Special Education, 30,* 264–275. doi:10.1177/088840640703000406

Potthoff, D., & Alley, R. (1996). Selecting placement sites for student teachers and pre-student teachers: Six considerations. *The Teacher Educator, 32,* 85–98. doi:10.1080/08878739609555135

Pretti-Frontczak, K., Giallourakis, A., Janas, D., & Hayes, A. (2002). Using a family-centered preservice curriculum to prepare early intervention and early childhood special education personnel. *Teacher Education and Special Education, 25,* 291–297. doi:10.1177/088840640202500308

Sewell, T. (2012). Are we adequately preparing teachers to partner with families? *Early Childhood Education Journal, 40,* 259–263. doi:10.1007/s10643-011-0503-8

15

Principles of Universal Design for Learning to Encourage Self-Determination for Parents With Intellectual Disabilities

RUTH A. FALCO
LESLIE J. MUNSON
CAITLIN SEIFERT
Portland State University

As Katie, an Early Head Start home visitor, drove to her next home visit, she thought about the complexities of this family. Crystal was a 27-year-old single mom who experienced intellectual disabilities (ID). She lived with her son, Scott, age 2, and her mother, Sharon. According to information shared by her mother, Crystal was identified as having ID when she was in elementary school.

Katie was finding it difficult to develop a relationship with Crystal. Crystal was usually silent and responded to direct questions with one or two words. Katie wondered if Crystal feared that her ability to parent would be called into question. She knew Crystal had a history of two investigations by Department of Human Services (DHS) and was still under scrutiny by the agency. Crystal's mother watched Katie's first two home visits very attentively.

Katie observed that Crystal was committed to parenting Scott and had many parenting strengths. According to her mother, Crystal independently maintained a consistent routine for Scott while she was away at work and took him on the bus to the relief nursery preschool class three days a week. Additionally, she took Scott on walks to a shopping mall and local playgrounds.

Katie felt that DEC Recommended Family Practices (2014) provided valuable guidance for her work with this complex family. Thus, she worked on building a trusting and respectful relationship with Crystal (F1), providing information to Crystal in ways she would understand (F2), responding to Crystal's concerns and priorities (F3), empowering her in making choices about intervention goals and activities (F4), and helping Crystal strengthen her interaction with Scott to address his developmental needs (F5 and F6).

> An essential part of building a positive relationship involves the service provider demonstrating respect for the parent with ID as a self-determined adult.

Through the first half of the 20th century, it was not considered appropriate for individuals with ID to have sexual relations or become parents (Feldman, 2010). However, during the last half of the 20th and in the 21st century, awareness increased that, regardless of societal beliefs, growing numbers of people with intellectual disabilities were becoming parents and often needed support. Unfortunately, parents with ID continue to be at greater risk than other parents of losing their children through child-protection court proceedings and the assumption of their incompetence as parents (National Council on Disability [NCD], 2012). These risks are often confounded with other risk factors, such as poverty, the educational level of parents, stress, depression, and other health issues.

With the growing number of parents with ID, most home visitors, such as early intervention personnel, health workers, and others, will encounter these parents in their work. Research indicates positive outcomes for parents with ID and their children when education and support are provided (Coren, Thomae, & Hutchfield, 2011; Feldman, 2010; Wade, Llewellyn, & Matthews, 2008). Thus, service providers require effective methods to assist parents with ID to be competent parents.

Guidelines for services to all families, as seen in the DEC Recommended Practices (2014), provide a framework to apply as home visitors and others serve parents with ID. While all the Family recommended practices are important, we focus here on the theme of "family-centered practices," particularly F1, F2, F3, F4, F5 and F6 (p. 10).

The role of self-determination in building trusting, respectful, and responsive partnerships with parents with ID (F1 and F3). Parents with ID are often wary of service providers because they and their families are aware of the risk of losing their children through child-protection court proceedings (NCD, 2012). This awareness can create barriers between families with ID and service providers. Yet, it is possible to build supportive and trusting relationships. An essential part of building a positive relationship involves the service provider demonstrating respect for the parent with ID as a self-determined adult. As described by Wehmeyer (2005), "self-determined behavior refers to volitional actions that enable one to act as the primary causal agent in one's life" (p. 117). Self-determination involves "people self-directing their lives in positive ways" (Nonnemacher & Bambara, 2011, p. 327). In a qualitative study, Nonnemacher and Bambara (2011) found that adults with ID described service providers as supportive of self-determination when they were trustworthy, developed quality interpersonal relationships, and provided information to support, rather than control or judge, decision-making and competence. For example, the home visitor can use strategies to fully involve parents in choosing goals for their child and themselves, determining activities to achieve those goals, and evaluating success in achieving the goals. Table 1 shows the relationship between principles of self-determination and the Family recommended practices.

After two home visits with Crystal and Scott, now was the time to establish goals. Katie identified strengths and concerns by using the information from

Table 1
Guidelines for Providing Services to Parents With ID

DEC Recommended Practices	Self-determination	Universal Design for Learning
F1 Practitioners build trusting and respectful partnerships with the family through interactions that are sensitive and responsive to cultural, linguistic, and socioeconomic diversity.	• Demonstrate respect for the parent with ID as a self-determined adult. • Develop a quality interpersonal relationship with the parent.	• Build on the parents' strengths and preferences.
F2 Practitioners provide the family with up-to-date, comprehensive, and unbiased information in a way that they can understand and use to make informed choices and decisions.	• Provide information to support, rather than control or judge, decision-making and competence. • Provide opportunities, supports, and accommodations for self-determined behavior.	• Use multiple means of representation (spoken, written, pictures, graphics, video). • Model new skills.
F3 Practitioners are responsive to the family's concerns, priorities, and changing life circumstances.	• Empower the parent to make choices and decisions. • Encourage the parent to choose goals based upon their own perceptions of what they and their child need.	• Respond to the parent's preferences and interests. • Respond to the parent's concerns and needs.
F4 Practitioners and the family work together to create outcomes or goals, develop individualized plans, and implement practices that address the family's priorities and concerns and the child's strengths and needs.	• Focus on goals chosen by the parent. • Encourage the parent to choose activities for practicing new skills based on their interests and their child's interests.	• Ask the parent what types of information work best for them. • Focus on how improvements in parenting skills are related to the child's development.
F5 Practitioners support family functioning, promote family confidence and competence, and strengthen family-child relationships by acting in ways that recognize and build on family strengths and capacities.	• Offer multiple ways to use new skills and support the parent to try out new skills in the ways they prefer.	• Use visuals and the family's technology (e.g., cell phone or tablet) to prompt practice of new skills.
F6 Practitioners engage the family in opportunities that support and strengthen parenting knowledge and skills and parenting competence and confidence in ways that are flexible, individualized, and tailored to the family's preferences.	• Encourage the parent to choose goals and to choose activities for practicing skills leading to the goals. • Empower the parent to evaluate progress toward goals.	• Consistently focus on parent and child goals in each home visit. • Provide specific, positive feedback; descriptive praise; and encouragement in forms the parent appreciates.

developmental testing of Scott, her own observations, Crystal's responses to questions, her video recordings of interactions between Scott and Crystal, discussions with Scott's teacher, and scores from the Parenting Interactions with Children: Checklist of Observations Linked to Outcomes (PICCOLO; Roggman, Cook, Innocenti, Jump Norman, & Christiansen, 2013). Crystal's strengths in interactions with Scott included her physical proximity and attention to him, her provision of materials for play, and her attempts to interact. Concerns included Crystal's limited use of verbal language and positive facial expressions to engage Scott. Scott's developmental strengths were in motor and cognitive areas. The main concern was his language development. From these identified strengths and concerns, Katie had a few ideas for possible goals to discuss with Crystal.

Katie had observed that Crystal used visual and verbal information better than written information, so she planned to present ideas for goals in pictures

with simple verbal descriptions. She also planned to use the video recordings to show Crystal positive examples of possible goals. She chose images that represented "Smile at your child" and "Talk more to your child." Katie wondered what goal Crystal would choose. She realized that to encourage Crystal's development of self-determination, she must respect her choice of goals.

After Katie and Crystal discussed possible goals, Crystal wanted to increase the times that she and Scott had fun together. So, she chose the behavior of "Smile at your child." Katie emphasized that by smiling more when Scott looked at her, Crystal could encourage him to pay attention to her when playing and doing other routines.

Applying Universal Design for Learning (UDL) when providing services to parents with ID (F2, F4, F5, F6). Universal Design for Learning (UDL) provides "a framework to improve and optimize learning for all people" (CAST, n.d.). UDL serves as a foundational approach for support to parents with ID. Through applying UDL principles, practitioners can provide "up-to-date, comprehensive and unbiased information in a way that the family can understand and use to make informed choices and decisions" (DEC, 2014, p. 10). Table 1 provides a guide for the application of UDL principles. UDL principles are applied in supporting parents with ID to expand their parenting skills by (a) using multiple modes to provide information (words, pictures, video examples, modeling); (b) encouraging multiple ways for using new skills and supporting the parent to try out new skills in the ways that they prefer; and (c) supporting motivation through multiple means, based upon the parents' preferences and interests. When these principles are applied within the context of a trusting and respectful relationship, parents with ID can build on their strengths and expand their positive parenting abilities.

Use Multiple Modes to Provide Information

Multiple modes of presentation (CAST, n.d.) make it more likely that information will be provided in a way all parents, including those with ID, will understand. Limitations in literacy, language comprehension, and expression are common concerns for adults with ID and other learning disabilities. These concerns can be addressed through use of multiple modes of communication.

Parents with ID benefit when written and spoken information is provided in clear and simple language and when service providers use ordinary, everyday language (appropriate for their culture and background) while avoiding professional jargon. When sharing written information with parents who have ID, the use of short, straightforward sentences and simple, consistent vocabulary will help the parent understand (Wade et al., 2008).

Model and use visuals. Because of limitations in receptive understanding of language and a stronger aptitude for visual learning, parents with ID may also benefit when service providers show what they mean visually in addition to explaining verbally (Wade et al., 2008). Providing a clear demonstration or modeling may be helpful. Pictures and other graphics that clearly represent a concept or action also help adults with ID to understand information that is presented orally or in writing. Pictorial representations of information also can help adults with ID to remember and apply the information at the appropriate time and place (Mechling & Gustafson, 2009). Visuals also provide an effective strategy to support working memory and promote completion of a series of behaviors. For example, a picture activity schedule could be used to show the planned activities for a home visit to the parent with ID, or simple line drawings could be used to show the steps that are necessary for a parenting activity, such as bathing the child. Visuals may also be useful to parents with ID in the process of decision-making to show and compare available options. Additionally, simple narrative stories, similar to social stories, can combine pictures and words to describe a new skill and provide multiple examples of its application.

Video representations, including recordings of behaviors in the natural environment or staged recordings to show specific aspects of new skills, help parents with ID to understand. These types of video presentations were demonstrated to be effective in parenting education for a variety of families (Benzies et al., 2013). Additionally, adults with intellectual disabilities have successfully used video models in learning a variety of skills (Mechling & Gustafson, 2009).

Combining multiple modes of representation, such as modeling, pictures, and video, helps all learners, especially those with ID and other learning difficulties (CAST, n.d.). And, the home visitor may observe or the parent may be able to identify which types of information work best for them. For example, one parent may indicate that modeling by the home visitor is the best way to learn, while another parent may indicate that they prefer watching a video or reading

Parents with ID benefit when written and spoken information is provided in clear and simple language and when service providers use ordinary, everyday language.

a narrative story with their child and the home visitor. Parents with ID and their children will benefit when service providers choose means of representation to use in sharing information that the parent readily understands. Careful consideration of how much information to present at one time will also benefit parents with ID (Wade et al., 2008). Breaking down complex information and presenting one new piece of information at a time accommodates difficulties of working memory and avoids information overload.

Katie considered several ways to use pictures to communicate the goal of "smiling more." She captured a picture in which Crystal was smiling at Scott from the initial video recording. They posted this picture in the photo gallery on Crystal's cell phone and in Scott's bedroom. With Crystal's permission, Katie decided to video-record Crystal and Scott playing during each home visit. Then, she would show the video to Crystal and they could identify positive examples of Crystal smiling at Scott and reflect on Scott's reactions. Katie realized that it would be best to focus on just one new goal at a time with Crystal and show her examples of that skill through multiple modes.

Breaking down complex information and presenting one new piece of information at a time accommodates difficulties of working memory and avoids information overload.

Encourage Multiple Ways for Parents to Use New Skills

A second UDL principle involves multiple ways for individuals to act on or express what they learned (CAST, n.d.). Home visitors can encourage parents to try out new behaviors in ways that work for them and that they prefer. For example, if the goal is for parents to get in a face-to-face position to interact with their child, some parents may prefer to do this while seated on the floor with their child, some may prefer to be seated on the couch, and some may prefer to begin this type of interaction with the child seated in an infant seat or high chair. The home visitor or other service provider can model several ways to do a new skill or show more than one video model and invite the parent to choose a way to try. When given the opportunity to choose a way to do a new behavior, the parent will be more likely to find a way to apply the behavior that will work for them and their child, and they may use the behavior more often.

Encourage and prompt practice. Parents with ID may need repeated practice in using new skills (Wade et al., 2008). Service providers can provide practice and review of the new skills during each home visit. Effective prompts, including verbal, gestural, and gentle physical guidance, respectfully provided, can help the parent with ID apply a new skill successfully (Feldman, 2010; Wade et al., 2008). Visual supports, such as photos on the parent's phone (Wade et al., 2008) or graphics posted in the home, can also be tried to facilitate practice when the service provider is not present.

Use technology. Technology can be used to prompt parents to practice new skills (Wade et al., 2008). For example, a cell phone with an appointment calendar can remind a parent to include play times with their child during the day. If a parent has access to a more elaborate device, such as a tablet or smart phone, an application for providing a visual schedule could be added on that device to provide prompting for practice. Simple text messages can also be sent by the service provider to remind the parent to use their new skills.

Support Motivation by Multiple Means

Support to parents with ID to learn new skills should address motivation for acquisition, generalization, and maintenance of the new skills (Knowles, Machalicek, & Van Norman, 2015). UDL principles (CAST, n.d.) indicate that when activities are responsive to the learner's preferences and interests, all aspects of learning are enhanced.

Incorporate choice. Motivation can be enhanced by involving parents in choosing their goals and daily routines and activities to practice that can lead to new skills. Learning a new skill within the context of a familiar and enjoyable activity should enhance the parent's success. Offering choices on how to receive information (e.g., written or picture handouts or videos) may also enhance motivation. Opportunities to make choices were identified as important to self-determination and quality of life for people with intellectual disabilities (Walker et al., 2011).

Address parent's concerns. Relevance to the parent's concerns and perceived needs may also enhance motivation. Parents may be motivated to focus attention on improving routines that are challenging to them, especially if parenting skills for these routines can be broken down into small steps that can be successfully accomplished.

Provide positive feedback. Acknowledging improved use of a new skill provides incentives for the parent to continue its use. Positive feedback and encouragement are two effective forms of positive motivation for use with parents with ID. Ample research demonstrates that positive feedback following the use of new behaviors increases the likelihood they will continue and increase (Feldman, 2010). However, it is important to understand that positive feedback may differ across people. For example, some adults appreciate social praise from others while some individuals find praise to be embarrassing and uncomfortable.

Home visitors can observe the parent's responses to feedback to identify the type of feedback that is most appreciated by the parent. Whenever giving positive feedback, it is most effective to describe the specific behavior in a way that the parent will clearly understand, such as "you are smiling at Scott." Additionally, the home visitor can help the parent recognize positive responses from the child when they use the new skill. In this example, the home visitor might say, "Look at how he was watching you when you smiled." Focusing on the child's growth may also enable the parent to see how improvements in their parenting skills are related to changes in their child's development.

After Katie and Crystal watched the video together, Katie invited Crystal to practice her goal of smiling at Scott. Crystal chose using the new sidewalk chalk for the practice activity. This gave Katie opportunities to suggest ways to get Scott's attention, encourage Crystal's smiling, and point out Scott's positive reactions. During the activity, Katie gave positive feedback to Crystal by saying "he likes that smile" when Crystal smiled and Scott smiled back.

To support Crystal's practice of the new interaction behavior between home visits, Katie used pictures captured from the videos to make a narrative story that described multiple examples of her smiling at Scott during play and other activities. The story shared Scott's point of view and described his pleasure when she smiled at him. She suggested that Crystal and Scott look at the storybook together between their weekly home visits.

During her home visit, Katie took several pictures on Crystal's phone that showed Crystal smiling at Scott during activities. These included pictures of her smiling while helping him put on his coat, while using sidewalk chalk with him outdoors, and while sharing a snack with him when they came back inside. Katie hoped the gallery of pictures on her phone would remind Crystal to practice smiling at Scott during activities throughout the week.

At their next home visit, Katie reviewed the goal with Crystal and asked her about what was happening as she practiced fun activities with Scott and smiled at him more often. Crystal said she was smiling at Scott when they ate a snack together and he smiled in return. She smiled and reported, "He looks at me more."

Conclusion

Studies show that parents with ID can successfully care for their children if given adequate support and parent education (Feldman, 2010). To maximize support to parents with ID, service providers can combine the Family recommended practices (DEC, 2014, pp. 10–11) with approaches that support self-determination while using UDL principles. Refer to Table 1 for a quick reference to the application of principles of self-determination and UDL while applying the DEC Recommended Practices. Applying these principles and practices enables the home visitor to support parents with ID to achieve, apply, and maintain the parenting skills they need with confidence; strengthen their relationship with their child; and provide competent and successful care.

References

Benzies, K. M., Magill-Evans, J., Kurilova, J., Nettel-Aguirre, A., Blahitka, L., & Lacaze-Masmonteil, T. (2013). Effects of video modeling on the interaction skills of first-time fathers of late preterm infants. *Infants and Young Children, 26,* 333–348. doi:10.1097/IYC.0b013e3182a4ed5e

CAST. (n. d.). About universal design for learning. Retrieved from http://www.cast.org/udl/index.html

Coren, E., Thomae, M., & Hutchfield, J. (2011). Parenting training for intellectually disabled parents: A Cochrane systematic review. *Research on Social Work Practice, 21,* 432–441. doi:10.1177/1049731511399586

Division for Early Childhood. (2014). *DEC recommended practices in early intervention/early childhood special education 2014*. Retrieved from http://www.dec-sped.org/recommended practices

Feldman, M. (2010). Parenting education programs. In G. Llewellyn, R. Traustadóttir, D. McConnell, & H. B. Sigurjónsdóttir (Eds.), *Parents with intellectual disabilities: Past, present and futures* (pp. 119–136). London, England: John Wiley & Sons.

Knowles, C., Machalicek, W., & Van Norman, R. (2015). Parent education for adults with intellectual disability: A review and suggestions for future research. *Developmental Neurorehabilitation, 18*, 336–348. doi:10.3109/17518 423.2013.832432

Mechling, L. C., & Gustafson, M. (2009). Comparison of the effects of static picture and video prompting on completion of cooking related tasks by students with moderate intellectual disabilities. *Exceptionality, 17*, 103–116. doi:10.1080/09362830902805889

National Council on Disability. (2012). *Rocking the cradle: Ensuring the rights of parents with disabilities and their children.* Washington, DC: Author.

Nonnemacher, S. L., & Bambara, L. M. (2011). "I'm supposed to be in charge": Self-advocates' perspectives on their self-determination support needs. *Intellectual and Developmental Disabilities, 49*, 327–340. doi:10.1352/1934-9556-49.5.327

Roggman, L. A., Cook, G. A., Innocenti, M. S., Jump Norman, V., & Christiansen, K. (2013). *Parenting interactions with children: Checklist of observations linked to outcomes (PICCOLO) tool.* Baltimore, MD: Paul H. Brookes.

Wade, C., Llewellyn, G., & Matthews, J. (2008). Review of parent training interventions for parents with intellectual disability. *Journal of Applied Research in Intellectual Disabilities, 21*, 351–366. doi:10.1111/j.1468-3148.2008.00449.x

Walker, H. M., Calkins, C., Wehmeyer, M. L., Walker, L., Bacon, A., Palmer, S. B., ... Johnson, D. R. (2011). A social-ecological approach to promote self-determination. *Exceptionality, 19*, 6–18. doi:10.1080/09362835.2011.537220

Wehmeyer, M. L. (2005). Self-determination and individuals with severe disabilities: Re-examining meanings and misinterpretations. *Research and Practice for Persons With Severe Disabilities, 30*, 113–120. doi:10.2511/rpsd.30.3.113

16

Family Capacity-Building
Mediating Parent Learning Through Guided Video Reflection

Hannah H. Schertz
Kathryn Horn
Indiana University

THE DIVISION FOR EARLY CHILDHOOD'S RECOMMENDED PRACtices (2014) address three categories of family practices: family-centered practices, family and professional collaboration practices, and family capacity-building practices. Although the strategies we describe in this article incorporate all three, we focus particularly on capacity-building practices. Capacity-building practices are described as participatory-enhancing experiences with three central aims for parent learning: (a) strengthening existing knowledge and skills, (b) promoting new abilities, and (c) enhancing self-efficacy. This article introduces mediated learning as a framework to support family capacity building. This approach incorporates guided reflection on parent-child interaction to use parents' expertise, facilitate their new conceptual learning, and support their understanding of their capacity to support child learning. We describe specific mediated learning strategies and illustrate their use in two family examples. Although these practices were developed for families of toddlers with autism, they are transferrable to families of other toddlers with special needs, especially those related to social, cognitive, and communicative learning.

A majority of parents surveyed in early intervention (EI) programs reported no direct involvement in intervention activities (Dunst, Bruder, & Espe-Sherwindt, 2014). This finding, which parallels gaps in family-supportive EI practices (Campbell & Sawyer, 2009; Schertz, Baker, Hurwitz, & Benner, 2011), runs counter to the known positive impact of parent involvement on child outcomes, parent self-efficacy, and parent well-being (Trivette, Dunst, & Hamby, 2010). This pattern of underinvolvement may result from a lack of role clarity for parents in EI (Kemp & Turnbull, 2014; Sawyer & Campbell, 2012), underpreparation of personnel in family practices (Campbell, Chiarello, Wilcox, & Milbourne, 2009), and the failure to view parent-child interaction as impactful despite findings to the contrary (Hebbeler & Gerlach-Downie, 2002). This research/practice disparity calls for specific approaches to address the gap.

Mediated Learning: A Framework to Support Family Capacity

A number of EI approaches have incorporated a parent role in promoting infant and toddler learning, and some rely on parents replicating predetermined professionally devised strategies. A contrasting approach, building on Vygotsky's (1978) and Feuerstein's (1980) sociocultural theory, depicts learning as a process that is mediated or guided in natural social contexts. Klein (2003) applied mediated learning theory in her work with parents and infants with learning challenges to help parents "mediate" between what the child brings to the learning process and learning features of the environment.

Instead of training parents to focus on preprogrammed child skills, Klein (2003) aimed to support the learning process itself, an approach that demonstrated positive long-term effects on child outcomes. Klein used video recordings of parent-child interaction to build parents' capacity for using mediated learning principles to support child learning through high-quality interaction. The principles support both parents' and children's active engagement in the learning process to help them generate their own learning rather than passively responding to others.

Parents' ability to learn new skills is enhanced by their self-efficacy, defined as the perception of one's competence and learning potential (Bandura, 1982). Parent self-efficacy has been found to relate to the use of family-centered intervention practices (Dunst, Trivette, & Hamby, 2007), parent competence (Hess, Teti, & Hussey-Gardner, 2004), and positive child outcomes (Coleman & Karraker, 2003). These findings suggests a path in which facilitating parents' conceptual learning increases their competence to support child learning and allows them to see their efforts pay off in improved child outcomes, further strengthening their learning as their views of their competence are enhanced.

The strategies, drawn from our multiple research studies (Schertz, Odom, Baggett, & Sideris, 2013) and described and illustrated below, show the use of a mediated learning approach for toddlers with autism and their parents. The strategies vest parents with a central role in the intervention process by leveraging their expertise and bolstering their conceptual understanding of intervention content and process components. To summarize, the goal of mediated learning is to promote new abilities and strengthen existing knowledge and skills in ways that support self-efficacy through a strong parent leadership role.

In all aspects of the intervention, parents are viewed as bringing expertise derived from the strength of the parent-child relationship and from their family priorities, values, and traditions.

Strategies to Promote Family Capacity Through Mediated Learning

A brief description of the Joint Attention Mediated Learning (JAML) intervention is provided for context. Rather than a tightly defined protocol, JAML provides a framework to guide preverbal social communication learning for toddlers with autism and mediate parent and toddler learning of this content. Social communication is the core concern in autism and is linked to early challenges in attention to faces, reciprocal interaction, and joint attention (Schertz, Horn, Lee, & Mitchell, 2017). These focus areas translate into targeted outcomes and are ordered according to their appearance in typical development. Mediated learning principles are applied both to guide parent learning (the focus of this article) and to parents' guidance of toddler learning. During weekly home-based sessions, the early intervention provider (EIP) focuses on the parent rather than intervening directly with the child to emphasize the importance of the parent-child relationship as the preferred learning venue.

Five mediated learning principles are infused throughout the activities described below. These principles are (a) focusing (orienting parents toward salient aspects of parent-child interaction that support the phase of intervention), (b) organizing and planning (transmitting and translating new content systematically), (c) giving meaning (helping parents discriminate between aspects of interaction that are more and less effective and relevant to the current intervention emphasis), (d) encouraging (facilitating parents' recognition of their impact on the child's learning), and (e) expanding (engaging parents to add breadth and depth to interaction opportunities). The principles are exemplified in the family examples below.

In all aspects of the intervention, parents are viewed as bringing expertise derived from the strength of the parent-child relationship and from their family priorities, values, and traditions. Intervention activities, summarized in Table 1, are designed to foster the three components of family capacity building: strengthening existing knowledge and skills, promoting new abilities, and enhancing parenting self-efficacy.

Beginning with the first activity of the session (reviewing parents' reports of activities from the past week), parents take on a leadership role as the EIP listens. This activity, which recognizes the parent as the primary direct facilitator of the child's learning, focuses on parent self-efficacy by highlighting successes and identifying areas for additional support from the parent. The second activity, video-recorded parent-child interaction, again offers parents the floor, this time to showcase mediated learning strategies that support child engagement with a specific focus on the current targeted social communication outcome. This activity focuses on strengthening existing knowledge and skills while continuing to enhance self-efficacy.

The third activity, guided video reflection, elicits the parent's assessment of the child's success with the targeted outcome, the child's response to the parent's use of mediated learning principles, parent-generated questions, and ideas

Table 1
Roles and Mediated Learning Principles Linked to Early Intervention Activities

Activity	Purpose	Mediated learning principles applied	EIP role	Parent role	Family capacity-building emphasis
Review of previous week's activity	Review, identification of successes/ challenges	Focusing, organizing, and planning	Listener	Lead role: Reporter	Self-efficacy
Video-recorded parent-child interaction	Mediate child learning of targeted outcome	Focusing	Observer	Lead role: Implementer	Strengthening Self-efficacy
Guided video reflection	Reflectively assess parent mediation and child engagement	Focusing, giving meaning, encouraging, expanding	Shared lead: Facilitator	Shared lead: Reflector	Strengthening Self-efficacy
Presentation of new conceptual material with parent examples	Introduce new child outcomes and linked mediated learning principles	Focusing, organizing and planning, giving meaning, expanding	Lead role: Presenter	Observer, listener	New learning Self-efficacy
Activity planning for the coming week	Translate conceptual learning into daily plans	Focusing, organizing and planning, giving meaning	Shared role: Facilitator	Shared role: Translation to daily activities	Strengthening Self-efficacy
Translation into daily interactions	Integrate new concepts into everyday activities	Focusing, giving meaning, expanding	Background support	Lead role: Implementer	Strengthening Self-efficacy

Notes
Strengthening = Strengthening existing parenting knowledge and skills by harnessing their expertise
Self-efficacy = Enhancing parenting self-efficacy and leadership
New learning = Promoting new knowledge and skills

on adjustments parents might make. Self-efficacy and the strengthening of existing knowledge and skills are promoted as the parent is again encouraged to take the lead and the EIP asks and responds to questions and highlights child or parent successes the parent may have overlooked. As parents indicate what did not work as hoped, the EIP asks leading questions, referencing conceptual learning materials previously presented to facilitate reflection and the generation of new ideas and solutions. The EIP avoids taking on a didactic role or pointing out deficiencies, which are likely to emerge from the parents' reflection. As with the parents' review of the prior week's activities, these reflective strategies are intended to promote the parent's self-reliance.

The fourth activity, presentation of new material, is for promoting new abilities. The EIP assumes an overt teaching role while continuing to promote parent self-efficacy. This activity is explicitly conceptual in focus and provides new content knowledge to prepare parents to meaningfully translate concepts flexibly into everyday activities and routines. Once new material on intervention content (the targeted outcome) and process (mediated learning principles) is presented verbally and in print, examples of how other parents have translated the new concepts into parent-child interaction are presented as "Ideas Other Parents Have Used." These ideas are shared as printed lists and as video examples of other parents using mediated principles to address targeted outcomes with their toddlers who are also on the au-

tism spectrum. The purpose of using examples generated by other parents rather than EIP modeling or didactic instruction is to illustrate parents' capacity to support their children's learning creatively and in ways consistent with their unique preferences and circumstances. In assessing the intervention's acceptability, parents consistently identify these video examples as the most valuable component of the intervention because of the conceptual clarity they provide.

The fifth activity, translating insights from the video reflection and new conceptual learning into daily activity plans, brings the parent back into the lead as the EIP elicits and records parents' ideas on how the current targeted outcome might be encouraged in the coming week through planned parent-child interaction and in everyday activities and routines.

Again, strengthening existing knowledge and skills to enhance self-efficacy is the goal for this activity. Parent-generated ideas are elicited to affirm and incorporate their knowledge of their children's interests and aversions, their family priorities, and their cultural values and traditions. Because it is the parent rather than the EIP who generates these plans (albeit with EIP support), cultural mismatches are circumvented while parental competence and self-confidence are bolstered.

Finally, the parent, now armed with a firm conceptual understanding of the near-term intervention aims and mediated learning processes that can support them, implements planned activities throughout the week, exercising discretion and flexibility. Using a quick checkoff form, the parent keeps track of time spent, routines in which the intervention outcomes were addressed, a quick rating of the child's success, and any comments s/he wants to remember to share at the next session. Again, this activity is designed to strengthen existing learning and enhance self-efficacy.

Family Examples

Nadine and Bonnie

Nadine, a medical professional, is mother to 20-month-old Bonnie. Nadine and Bonnie are referred to Paula for early intervention. Bonnie is a pleasant child who communicates with a few single-syllable sounds, or she waits for others to guess what she needs or wants. Bonnie has strong sensory and repetitive interests, and she likes to play alone. At the intake interview, Nadine tells Paula that while Bonnie does not seem unhappy, Nadine longs to join her in play and

conversation. Nadine's priority is for her daughter to feel well-bonded to her, "like I feel with my own mother," which Paula acknowledges as a valuable and attainable goal.

In her intervention work with Paula, Nadine is developing ways to mediate Bonnie's learning to look at her face in a socially meaningful way. Paula explains that attending to faces is foundational to Nadine's "big picture" goal of making social connections. Paula uses the principle *focusing* to emphasize activities that helped Nadine encourage Bonnie's looks to her face as they review a log Nadine kept for the week. During the prior session, Nadine noted that Bonnie seemed bored, so Paula used the principle *expanding* to help Nadine develop richer activities that would better engage Bonnie. Nadine decided to plan activities that revolved around Bonnie's preference for physical and outdoor play, including "Ring Around the Rosie" and "Row, Row, Row Your Boat" games, playing on the swing set, and taking walks outside together. Nadine tells Paula that Bonnie liked all of the activities, and the outdoor activities were most useful in helping Bonnie learn to attend to her face.

For the video recording, Nadine chooses to engage Bonnie in the walk activity. Paula is silent as she records, which again helps Nadine focus on facilitating Bonnie's looks to her face, the most important part of their interactions for now. When they return to the house, Nadine and Paula review the video while Bonnie has a snack in her high chair. Nadine and Paula laugh at Bonnie's antics. Paula waits for Nadine to identify when her efforts to support Bonnie's learning were most effective. Rather than driving the review, Paula uses the principle *giving meaning* by asking leading questions to help Nadine think about and internalize why certain strategies worked better than others. Nadine notices that Bonnie looks to her face best when Nadine makes anticipatory sounds and calls her name softly. Paula agrees and uses the principle *encouraging* by acknowledging how well Nadine's strategy worked.

Next, Paula presents Nadine with new information she can use to help Bonnie learn to look at faces in more socially complex ways. Paula uses the principle *organizing and planning* to strategically highlight parent-generated ideas that focused on this outcome. Paula shares "Ideas Other Parents Have Used" and shows videos of other parents successfully using a variety of strategies to enhance their children's ability to attend to faces. Paula then uses the principle *focusing* to help Nadine choose activities that will help Bonnie achieve greater competency with the outcome in the coming week, and they make a brief written plan. At the next session, there is clear evidence of Nadine's successful mediation of Bonnie's learning as Bonnie looks to Nadine's face more freely, seeks her company frequently, and appears to enjoy the planned games.

Donna and Brian

Donna, a professional athlete, is mother to 28-month-old Brian. They are also referred to Paula for early intervention. Brian communicates his needs and desires by leading others by the hand. He strongly prefers highly predictable routines and repetitive activities. Brian is very assertive and likes to take charge of the interaction when he engages with others. At the intake interview, Donna tells Paula that she wants to more easily understand what Brian is thinking and to have fun, relaxed interactions. Another priority is for Brian to share the family's love of sports. Paula understands and acknowledges the importance of this goal for the family.

In her intervention work with Paula, Donna is developing strategies to help Brian with reciprocal social interaction. Paula explains that being able to participate in "back and forth" reciprocal social interaction is foundational to Donna's "big picture" goal of Brian enjoying sports with the family. As they review the log Donna has kept for the week, Paula uses the principle *focusing* to emphasize activities that enhance Brian's interactive play. Donna planned several reciprocal "back and forth" activities, including games of knocking caps off their heads, ball rolling, and clapping, which she reports went only "okay." Paula uses the principle *giving meaning* as she asks leading questions to help Donna identify which activities were most effective. Donna explains that while Brian loved the ball rolling and cap games, he was less enthusiastic about the clapping game. Paula uses the principle *expanding* to encourage Donna to generate new ideas to follow Brian's interests in order to more effectively engage him.

Donna chooses the ball-rolling game for the video recording, which Paula films silently to let Donna focus on her interaction with Brian. Donna allows Brian to set the agenda, and the game evolves to include changing places and positions. When Brian points to a car, Donna follows his lead into car play, which has previously been a solitary restrictive interest for Brian. This time, though, he is able to share the toy with Donna, playing back and forth a few times. Afterward, both Donna and Paula are excited to review the video while Brian plays alone with his car. Donna takes the initiative by first pointing out how naturally Brian plays back and forth with the ball and expresses delight in his new ability to share the car. Paula uses the principle *giving meaning* by asking leading questions that help Donna recognize that following Brian's lead enhanced his ability to engage in reciprocal play. Paula uses the principle *encouraging* when she points out how expertly Donna facilitated Brian's move from solitary car play into a more social form of back-and-forth reciprocal engagement.

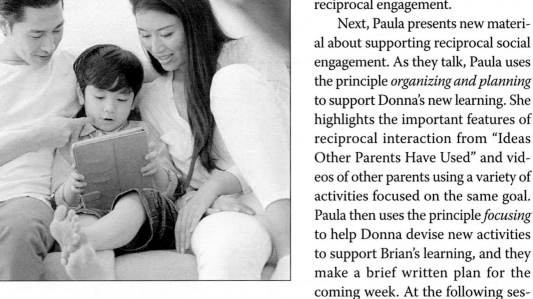

Next, Paula presents new material about supporting reciprocal social engagement. As they talk, Paula uses the principle *organizing and planning* to support Donna's new learning. She highlights the important features of reciprocal interaction from "Ideas Other Parents Have Used" and videos of other parents using a variety of activities focused on the same goal. Paula then uses the principle *focusing* to help Donna devise new activities to support Brian's learning, and they make a brief written plan for the coming week. At the following session, Donna sees clear evidence of success as Brian enthusiastically joins her in a reciprocal game of modified basketball. Paula makes a mental note that Donna's demeanor seems more positive this week and attributes this to her improved confidence in her ability to support Brian's learning.

Summary and Conclusions

The purpose of this article was to provide practical guidance on addressing the three prongs of family capacity building related to the DEC Recommended Practices: harnessing parents' expertise, promoting their new learning, and supporting self-efficacy. Mediated learning principles provide a framework for achieving these goals by vesting parents with a shared leadership role within a guided learning process. The five principles—focusing, organizing and planning, giving meaning, encouraging, and expanding—provide a structure for supporting parent learning systematically. The EIP embeds these principles in guided video reflection and other activities to help parents conceptualize content, empowering them to translate their new learning broadly throughout everyday parent-child interactions. The aim is to build parents' active engagement in the learning process rather than training them in prescribed intervention strategies. Although space does not permit a full description here, the same principles are applicable to parents' guidance of their children's learning. The mediated learning process for both parents and children share the goals of promoting engagement and a sense of order in the learning process, self-reliance, and motivation to actively and on their own initiative apply their learning in new situations.

References

Bandura, A. (1982). Self-efficacy mechanism in human agency. *American Psychologist, 37*, 122–147. doi:10.1037/0003-066X.37.2.122

Campbell, P. H., Chiarello, L., Wilcox, M. J., & Milbourne, S. (2009). Preparing therapists as effective practitioners in early intervention. *Infants & Young Children, 22*, 21–31. doi:10.1097/01.IYC.0000343334.26904.92

Campbell, P. H., & Sawyer, L. B. (2009). Changing early intervention providers' home visiting skills through participation in professional development. *Topics in Early Childhood Special Education, 28*, 219–234. doi:10.1177/0271121408328481

Coleman, P. K., & Karraker, K. H. (2003). Maternal self-efficacy beliefs, competence in parenting, and toddlers' behavior and developmental status. *Infant Mental Health Journal, 24*, 126–148. doi:10.1002/imhj.10048

Division for Early Childhood. (2014). *DEC recommended practices in early intervention/early childhood special education 2014*. Retrieved from http://www.dec-sped.org/recommendedpractices

Dunst, C. J., Bruder, M. B., & Espe-Sherwindt, M. (2014). Family capacity-building in early childhood intervention: Do context and setting matter? *School Community Journal, 24*(1), 37–48.

Dunst, C. J., Trivette, C. M., & Hamby, D. W. (2007). Meta-analysis of family-centered helpgiving practices research. *Mental Retardation and Developmental Disabilities Research Reviews, 13*, 370–378. doi:10.1002/mrdd.20176

Feuerstein, R. (1980). *Instrumental enrichment: An intervention program for cognitive modifiability*. Baltimore, MD: University Park Press.

Hebbeler, K. M., & Gerlach-Downie, S. G. (2002). Inside the black box of home visiting: A qualitative analysis of why intended outcomes were not achieved. *Early Childhood Research Quarterly, 17*, 28–51. doi:10.1016/s0885-2006(02)00128-x

Hess, C. R., Teti, D. M., & Hussey-Gardner, B. (2004). Self-efficacy and parenting of high-risk infants: The moderating role of parent knowledge of infant development. *Journal of Applied Developmental Psychology, 25*, 423–437. doi:10.1016/j.appdev.2004.06.002

Kemp, P., & Turnbull, A. P. (2014). Coaching with parents in early intervention: An interdisciplinary research synthesis. *Infants & Young Children, 27*, 305–324. doi:10.1097/iyc.0000000000000018

Klein, P. S. (2003). A mediational approach to early intervention: Israel. In S. L. Odom, M. J. Hanson, J. A. Blackman, & S. Kaul (Eds.), *Early intervention practices around the world* (pp. 69–80). Baltimore, MD: Paul H. Brookes.

Sawyer, B. E., & Campbell, P. H. (2012). Early interventionists' perspectives on teaching caregivers. *Journal of Early Intervention, 34*, 104–124. doi:10.1177/1053815112455363

Schertz, H. H., Baker, C., Hurwitz, S., & Benner, L. (2011). Principles of early intervention reflected in toddler research in autism spectrum disorders. *Topics in Early Childhood Special Education, 31*, 4–21. doi:10.1177/0271121410382460

Schertz, H. H., Horn, K., Lee, M., & Mitchell, S. (2017). Supporting parents to help toddlers with autism make social connections. *Young Exceptional Children, 20*(1), 16–29. doi:10.1177/1096250615576808

Schertz, H. H., Odom, S. L., Baggett, K. M., & Sideris, J. H. (2013). Effects of Joint Attention Mediated Learning for toddlers with autism spectrum disorders: An initial randomized controlled study. *Early Childhood Research Quarterly, 28,* 249–258. doi:10.1016/j.ecresq.2012.06.006

Trivette, C. M., Dunst, C. J., & Hamby, D. W. (2010). Influences of family-systems intervention practices on parent-child interactions and child development. *Topics in Early Childhood Special Education, 30,* 3–19. doi:10.1177/0271121410364250

Vygotsky, L. S. (1978). *Mind in society: The development of higher psychological processes.* Cambridge, MA: Harvard University Press.

17

Resources
to Support Family Practices

RASHIDA BANERJEE
University of Northern Colorado

FAMILY PRACTICES "REFER TO ONGOING ACTIVITIES THAT (1) PROMOTE the active participation of families in decision-making related to their child (e.g., assessment, planning, intervention); (2) lead to the development of a service plan (e.g., a set of goals for the family and child and the services and supports to achieve those goals); or (3) support families in achieving the goals they hold for their child and the other family members" (Division for Early Childhood, 2014, p.10). The Family recommended practices guide practitioners' interactions with the parents so practitioners can support parents to participate fully in all decision-making activities regarding their child and to support the development of parents' sense of competence and confidence in helping their child learn and grow (Trivette & Banerjee, 2015).

These resources supplement the articles in this monograph as well as extend additional important topics that were not covered. The first set of resources focuses on general information about working with families. The next three sets of resources are arranged according to the three themes found in the Family recommended practices: family-centered, family-capacity building, and family and professional collaboration (DEC, 2014). The last set of resources practitioners might find helpful to share with families. While there is content overlap among these categories, the tools and materials were categorized based on the primary goals of the resource. The resources consist of web-based information that is easily available and free.

The descriptions of resources have been summarized directly from the websites or documents to keep the information consistent with what was intended by the resource developers.

General Resources Related to Families

Child Maltreatment

This DEC position statement describes the roles of individuals and organizations in both prevention and intervention efforts to support young children with disabilities who have experienced maltreatment as well as their families. The action recommendations encompass explicit short-term and long-term goals in the following areas: practice, pre- and in-service preparation, research, and policy.

http://www.dec-sped.org/position-statements

DAP With Infants and Toddlers

The National Association for the Education of Young Children is a professional membership organization that works to promote high-quality early learning for all young children, birth through age 8, by connecting early childhood practice, policy, and research. The purpose of this position statement on developmentally appropriate practice with infants and toddlers is to promote excellence in supporting children birth to age 3 by providing a framework for best practice. Practice 5 describes ways professionals and programs are expected to partner with families.

https://www.naeyc.org/dap/infants-and-toddlers

ECTA Center Family Checklists

These performance checklists from the Early Childhood Technical Assistance Center are intended for practitioners (and leaders where noted) to increase their understanding and use of the DEC Family recommended practices and for self-evaluation of one's use of those practices.

http://ectacenter.org/decrp/topic-family.asp

The following checklists specifically cover the topic of Family recommended practices.

- **Family-Centered Practices Checklist**
  http://ectacenter.org/~pdfs/decrp/FAM-1_Fam-Ctrd_Practices_2017.pdf

- **Informed Family Decision-Making Practices Checklist**
  http://ectacenter.org/~pdfs/decrp/FAM-2_Inf_Family_Decision_2017.pdf

- **Family Engagement Practices Checklist**
  http://ectacenter.org/~pdfs/decrp/FAM-3_Fam_Engagement_2017.pdf

- **Family Capacity-Building Practices Checklist**
  http://ectacenter.org/~pdfs/decrp/FAM-4_Fam_Capacity-Building_2017.pdf

Engaging Diverse Families

These National Association for the Education of Young Children resources offer examples of successful family engagement practices. They provide resources for teachers and programs to successfully engage diverse families of all children in their programs.

https://www.naeyc.org/familyengagement

Family Culture, Values, and Language

This DEC position statement, *Responsiveness to ALL Children, Families, and Professionals: Integrating Cultural and Linguistic Diversity Into Policy and Practice*, explicitly addresses the implications of, and extends DEC's commitment to, culturally and linguistically responsive practices in early childhood.

http://www.dec-sped.org/position-statements

Family Enhancement Project

This webpage from the Puckett Institute provides a list of materials and activities that early intervention practitioners can use to promote their application of family assessment and intervention practices with parents of infants and toddlers with identified disabilities or developmental delays. The research-to-practice activities provide strategies that support and strengthen child, parent, and family development.

http://www.puckett.org/returns_investments_family_enhancement.php

Global Family Research Project

Subscribe to the blog from Global Family Research Project (previously Harvard Family Research Project) at the link below. The project connects research, policy, and practice to support a community of people dedicated to advancing children's learning and development.

https://globalfrp.org/#Subscribe

Head Start Parent, Family, and Community Engagement Framework

This framework is a research-based approach to program change designed to help Head Start programs achieve outcomes that lead to positive and enduring change for children and families.

https://eclkc.ohs.acf.hhs.gov/pdguide/media/resource_files/PFCEFramework.pdf

Where We Stand on Responding to Linguistic and Cultural Diversity

This National Association for the Education of Young Children position statement provides recommendations emphasizing that early childhood programs are responsible for creating a welcoming environment that respects diversity, supports children's ties to their families and community, and promotes both second-language acquisition and preservation of children's home languages and cultural identities. It states that linguistic and cultural diversity is an asset, not a deficit, for young children.

http://www.naeyc.org/files/naeyc/file/positions/diversity.pdf

Resources Related to Family-Centered Practices

Early Childhood Education Publications & Resources: Educator–Family Relationships

This webpage, developed by the Harvard Family Research Project, provides resources to engage families in community settings such as public libraries and during activities such as home visits to establish a family engagement system that extends throughout a child's life, supports children and families, and prepares children for success.

http://www.hfrp.org/early-childhood-education/
publications-resources?topic=42

The following specific resources also may be helpful:

- **The Home Visit Forum: Understanding and Improving the Role of Home Visitation**
  http://www.hfrp.org/early-childhood-education/
  publications-resources/the-home-visit-forum-understanding-and-
  improving-the-role-of-home-visitation

- **Creating Conditions for Effective and Ongoing Family Engagement**
  http://www.hfrp.org/early-child-
  hood-education/publications-resources/
  creating-conditions-for-effective-and-ongoing-family-engagement

- **Public Libraries: A Vital Space for Family Engagement**
  http://www.hfrp.org/early-child-
  hood-education/publications-resources/
  public-libraries-a-vital-space-for-family-engagement

Helping Young Children Who Have Experienced Trauma: Policies and Strategies for Early Care and Education

This report from Child Trends and the National Center for Children in Poverty describes early childhood trauma and its effects on young children and their families. It further offers promising strategies for early childhood programs and systems to help young children who have experienced trauma and their families and presents recommendations for state policymakers and other stakeholders looking to support trauma-informed early childhood educators for this vulnerable group.

https://www.childtrends.org/publications/ecetrauma/

Making the Match: Culturally Relevant Coaching and Training for Early Childhood Caregivers

The author of this article describes a study that explored practices critical to culturally responsive coaching for practitioners in early care settings. The journal provides additional free peer-reviewed articles on various early childhood topics.

http://ecrp.illinois.edu/v14n2/kruse.html

Talks on Tuesdays

Talks on Tuesdays are one-hour webinars designed to provide free online professional development opportunities on important topics in early intervention. Topics chosen for the Talks on Tuesdays webinar series are based on feedback from early intervention practitioners about what they wish to know more about.

http://veipd.org/main/talks_tuesdays.html

The following are examples of webinars that discuss working with families. (Web addresses take you to a list of talks for an entire year. Scroll down to find the specific topic.)

- **Tying the Knot: Engaging Families Beyond the Visit**
  http://veipd.org/main/sub_2013_talks_tuesdays.html

- **Unpacking Our Biases in Early Intervention**
  http://veipd.org/main/sub_2017_talks_tuesdays.html

- **Engaging Families During Visits: How to Engage Families During Visits So They Know What to Do Between Visits**
  http://veipd.org/main/sub_2015_talks_tuesdays.html

Resources Related to Family Capacity-Building Practices

Building Capacity and Welcoming Practices in Military-Connected Schools

This initiative by the University of Southern California formulates welcoming practices to help military children transition more easily in military-connected schools. This website provides tools for educators and administrators of PreK–12 schools to create welcoming and effective transition procedures that give students a successful start at their new school. There also are several videos that highlight how some schools have celebrated and supported their military-connected children.

http://buildingcapacity.usc.edu/

Coaching in Early Intervention

This webpage from the Virginia Early Intervention Professional Development Center provides links to multiple resources such as webinars, articles, websites, and audio/video modules to help practitioners during early intervention visits to support parents to develop their abilities to interact with their children in ways that support their child's development.

http://www.veipd.org/main/sub_coaching.html

Home Visiting: Supporting Parents and Child Development

This webpage from Zero to Three provides an array of resources and tools that are intended to help policymakers and professionals understand the importance of investing in home visiting programs and supporting the implementation of home visiting programs as part of a comprehensive and coordinated system of services for young children and their families.

https://www.zerotothree.org/resources/series/
home-visiting-supporting-parents-and-child-development

The National Child Traumatic Stress Network

The network's goal is to improve access to care, treatment, and services for traumatized children and adolescents exposed to traumatic events. The website provides multiple resources for professionals, families, and communities. Resources for families include definition and symptoms of trauma, support for families to cope with stress and trauma, and links to resources to help children and families better understand what they are feeling when they (or someone close to them) has experienced a traumatic event.

http://www.nctsn.org/resources/audiences/parents-caregivers

What Parents Have to Teach Us About Their Dual Language Children

The author of this article from the *Young Children* journal provides guidance to practitioners for collecting and understanding parent knowledge about their children who are dual language learners to enhance classroom practice.

http://www.naeyc.org/yc/article/
What-Parents-Have-to-Teach-Us-About-Their-Dual-Language-Children

Resources Related to Family and Professional Collaboration

Beach Center on Disability and Family Studies

The center focuses on developing measures on such topics as family quality of life and family-professional partnerships, family support policies such as person-directed funding and choice and control, the impacts of family support programs such as parent-to-parent and family-centered service coordination models, as well as training and support for practitioners serving families and their children with disabilities. This webpage includes tools such as a Family Quality of Life Survey, a Family Professional Partnership Survey, and a Family Community Integration Survey that can be used by practitioners and leaders for self-reflection and assessment.

http://beachcenter.org/families

Center for Appropriate Dispute Resolution in Special Education (CADRE)

The center encourages the use of mediation, facilitation, and other collaborative processes as strategies for resolving disagreements between parents and schools about children's educational programs and support services. CADRE supports parents, educators, administrators, attorneys, and advocates to benefit from the full continuum of dispute resolution options that can prevent and resolve conflict and ultimately lead to informed partnerships that focus on results for children and youth.

http://www.cadreworks.org/

CONNECT Modules

Using a five-step process, these learning modules are designed for faculty and professional development providers to use as they support practitioners and students in enhancing their work with young children and families. Practitioners can receive CEUs for participating in these modules. The following two modules provide strategies for positive family-professional collaboration:

- **Module 3: Communication for Collaboration**
  http://community.fpg.unc.edu/connect-modules/learners/module-3

- **Module 4: Family-Professional Partnerships**
  http://community.fpg.unc.edu/connect-modules/learners/module-4

Head Start's Parent, Family, and Community Engagement Simulations

Head Start's set of simulations helps professionals explore and practice everyday strategies to develop positive goal-oriented relationships with families. In Simulation 1, professionals can practice building bonds with families, beginning with an intake visit. Simulation 2 explores the process of developing and implementing goals with families. Simulation 3 explores using strengths-based attitudes to partner with families during challenging times.

https://eclkc.ohs.acf.hhs.gov/hslc/tta-system/family/pfce_simulation

Helping Military Families Transition From an IFSP to an IEP

This helpful video gives tips and pointers for professionals working with military families as they transition from Part C to Part B services. This website also has additional videos and resources developed by faculty and staff from several universities who work collaboratively to encourage issue-driven, learner-centered, collaborative programming for military service members and their families.

https://militaryfamilies.extension.org/2016/03/02/helping-military-families-transition-from-an-ifsp-to-an-iep/

Resources for Professionals to Offer to Families

Center on the Developing Child

The center at Harvard University conducts scientific research that informs policy and practices including the testing, implementation, and refinement of strategies designed to achieve significantly better life outcomes for children facing adversity. The website provides numerous resources on diverse topics such as brain development, executive function and regulation, toxic stress, and resilience. Professionals can share these evidence-based resources with families who want to learn more about how to support their young children's development.

http://developingchild.harvard.edu/

Family Equality Council

The Family Equality Council connects, supports, and represents the 3 million parents who are lesbian, gay, bisexual, and transgender in the United States and their 6 million children. The website provides resources for families that can also be used to inform professionals.

http://www.familyequality.org/

Meeting the Needs of Families With Young Children Experiencing and At Risk of Homelessness

This website from the U.S. Department of Health and Human Services provides resources on supporting children and their families who are experiencing homelessness. It includes guidance documents, self-assessment tools, and strategies to support access to housing and child care for families.

https://www.acf.hhs.gov/ecd/resource/ccdf-ch

My Baby's Hearing: Resources for Professionals

This website includes a variety of downloadable PDF documents that are intended for use with parents of children who are deaf or hard of hearing.

https://www.babyhearing.org/Audiologists/parent/index.asp

Parent to Parent USA

Parent to Parent USA (P2P USA) is a national nonprofit organization that promotes excellence in P2P programs across the nation and connects all statewide P2P programs nationally. Since the 1970s, P2P programs have been providing emotional and informational support to families. Readers are encouraged to check out Parent to Parent programs in their state.

http://www.p2pusa.org/

PracticedMind for Mindful Parenting

PracticedMind is a mindfulness and meditation coach for parents. This app is developed by IRIS Educational Media and is available for Android and IOS. There's also a YouTube video that describes mindful parenting.

http://www.practicedparenting.com/

https://www.youtube.com/watch?v=rQF719jij-A&feature=youtu.be

WonderBaby: Resources for Families of Children With Visual Impairments

This project, sponsored by Perkins School for the Blind, helps parents of young children with visual impairments as well as children with multiple disabilities. The website provides a database of articles written by parents who want to share with others what they have learned about playing with and teaching a child with visual impairments, as well as links to meaningful resources and ways to connect with other families.

http://www.wonderbaby.org/about

Wrightslaw

Wrightslaw provides accurate, reliable information about special education law, education law, and advocacy for children with disabilities for parents, educators, advocates, and attorneys. This website has numerous articles, cases, and resources that families may find useful.

http://www.wrightslaw.com/

Zero to Three: Parent Favorites

Zero to Three is a professional organization that works to promote high-quality early learning for infants and toddlers. This webpage provides a collection of its highest trending resources for parents and includes topics such as social-emotional development, sleep, brain development, and early learning.

https://www.zerotothree.org/resources/series/parent-favorites

References

Division for Early Childhood. (2014). *DEC recommended practices in early intervention/early childhood special education 2014.* Retrieved from http://www.dec-sped.org/recommendedpractices

Trivette, C. M., & Banerjee, R. (2015). Family: Using the recommended practices to build parent competence and confidence. In *DEC recommended practices: Enhancing services for young children with disabilities and their families* (DEC Recommended Practices Monograph Series No. 1; pp. 66–75). Los Angeles, CA: Division for Early Childhood.

18

Editorial Team

Editors

Carol M. Trivette, *East Tennessee State University*
Bonnie Keilty, *Hunter College, City University of New York*

Resources Within Reason

Rashida Banerjee, *University of Northern Colorado*

Reviewers

Betsy Ayankoya, *University of North Carolina at Chapel Hill*
Rashida Banerjee, *University of Northern Colorado*
Michael Barla, *Fontbonne University*
Ann Bingham, *University of Nevada, Reno*
Patricia Blasco, *Western Oregon University*
Deborah Bruns, *Southern Illinois University*
Kerry Bull, *Noah's Ark Australia*
Ted Burke, *Beyond the Box, Hawaii*
Sue Carbary, *Bank Street College of Education*
Deborah Chen, *California State University, Northridge*
Dana Childress, *Virginia Commonwealth University*
Vivian Correa, *University of North Carolina at Charlotte*
Ann Cox, *University of North Carolina at Chapel Hill*
Sharon Darling, *Florida Atlantic University*
Frances Davis, *Family, Infant, and Preschool Program, North Carolina*
Laurie Dinnebeil, *University of Toledo*
Karen Engel, *parent of a child with a disability, The Graduate Center and
    Hunter College, City University of New York*
Marilyn Espe-Sherwindt, *Kent State University*
Alyssa Fiss, *Mercer University*
John Forster, *parent of a child with a disability, Noah's Ark Australia*
Lise Fox, *University of Southern Florida*
Chelsea Guillen, *University of Illinois at Urbana-Champaign*
Gabriel Guyton, *Bank Street College of Education*
Shana Haines, *University of Vermont*
William Henninger, *University of Northern Iowa*
Mark Innocenti, *Utah State University*
Melissa Jackson, *Hunter College, City University of New York*
Erin Kinavey Wennerström, *University of Oregon*

Index

translating insights into daily interactions, *128t*, 129
traumatic stress, 69, 138, 140

unhealthy attachment, 69
unilateral decision-making, 77–78, *78t*, 79–80
Universal Design for Learning (UDL), *117t*, 118–122

video feedback, 17–18
video models, 119–120
video reflection, guided, 127–132, *128t*
video-recorded parent-child interactions, 17–18, 20,
          64, 120, 127–132, *128t*
visuals, 119–120

word use in decision-making, 76–77, 79–83
written feedback, 17